Crystal Power

Crystal Power

manifest happiness and wellbeing by harnessing the energy of crystals

MARY LAMBERT

CICO BOOKS

LONDON NEW YORK

First published in 2005 as *Crystal Energy*
This edition published in 2024 by CICO Books
An imprint of Ryland Peters & Small Ltd
20–21 Jockey's Fields   341 E 116th St
London WC1R 4BW   New York, NY 10029

www.rylandpeters.com

10 9 8 7 6 5 4 3 2 1

A CIP catalog record for this book is available from the Library of Congress
and the British Library.

ISBN: 978-1-80065-320-7

Printed in China

Designer: Jerry Goldie
Project editor: Liz Dean
Photography: Geoff Dann
Illustrations: Trina Dalziel

Safety Note
Please note that while the descriptions of the properties of some crystals refer to healing
benefits, they are not intended to replace diagnosis of illness or ailments, or healing or
medicine. Always consult your doctor or other health professional in the case of illness.

Contents

Introduction

For centuries, crystals have fascinated people. Prized for their beauty, these special stones adorn royalty and the rich and powerful, and continue to be revered for their spiritual and healing properties.

Crystals were formed millions of years ago when hot gases and mineral solutions rose to the surface from the molten layer of the earth. As they cooled, the atoms merged into patterns and three-dimensional lattices to become the crystals we know today. The special structure of a crystal lets it absorb, strengthen, and transmit electromagnetic energy that can heal and energize.

Crystals in ancient times

In the mythical city of Atlantis the colored rays from crystals treated physical and emotional illness. A great healing temple was thought to have existed in Atlantis, with a large circular room and domed ceiling made of interlocking crystals. These crystals were arranged to form ancient symbols that created patterns of color when illuminated by light. Around the room were separate healing rooms for illness and emotional healing, with vast crystal doors that were energized with the color needed for the patient.

Egyptian remains indicate that this ancient race also had rooms in their temples for treating patients with healing gemstones. The ancient Egyptian people understood the power of crystals, and their rulers, the pharaohs, wore stones such as malachite in their headdresses to bring wisdom. Tiger's eye, carnelian, and turquoise were shaped into amulets; shields, hearts, and scarabs were buried with the owner in their tomb to guide them on their last journey.

Crystal skulls

One of the most fascinating crystal finds was the discovery of anatomically perfect natural quartz crystal skulls, estimated to be at least 20,000 years old. One of the best-known skulls was discovered by Anna Mitchell-Hedges with her father, Frederick Albert Mitchell-Hedges, an archaeologist, in 1924 in the Mayan ruins of Lubaantum (however, others say that they purchased it at a London auction). No one knows why the skulls are here, but they incite mystical and spiritual happenings, and reportedly many people's lives have changed after contact with a skull. Quartz doesn't decay and because of its amplifying ability, some believe that the skulls are a kind of storage device for important cosmic knowledge.

Crystals today

In this book are 150 practical tips showing you how crystals can heal and energize the many different areas of your life. Both rough and polished crystals (see below) are used. They can look quite different, so choose the type that appeals to you.

In the home, crystals give you protection from any negative energies existing there. Lepidolite is a versatile stone to position in the living room as it absorbs electromagnetic emissions from electrical equipment or other sources. Different crystals stimulate the atmosphere and energy flow, making your home a more sociable place. Even an ailing house-plant responds to the special vibration of a piece of green tourmaline. At work, you can achieve success with the crystal energy of golden topaz and keep internet viruses at bay by circling malachite around your computer. Personal power is important and comes via our seven energy centers: the chakras. The unique vibration of a sodalite crystal, for instance, can stimulate your Third eye chakra, improving your intuitive abilities.

Everyone wants romance in their lives, and crystals with a loving vibration draw in a partner or improve a relation-ship. Rhodochrosite, a pretty pink and black stone, can help attract that desired soulmate. Crystal jewelry can also work on desires. Wearing a crystal pendant or earrings daily for a week or so allows the gems' intrinsic properties to make your dreams come true or resolve a current unhappiness.

When you use a crystal for physical and emotional healing, the crystal's vibration tunes in to the malfunctioning emissions of the organ or energetic area and gently corrects them, making you feel healthier and re-energized. Placing blue calcite on the skin, for example, is thought to help relieve the inflammation and itching of eczema, while natural quartz's strong energetic field releases long-held emotional fears.

Finally, our astrological star signs will always fascinate us, and many of us live up to some of the less pleasant traits associated with them. So if you know you are an impatient Gemini, use a sunny citrine to keep your restlessness under control or, as a Capricorn, you can dispel depressive tendencies with chalcedony.

These nurturing, beautiful companions heal and enhance your life and, if necessary, may leave you and move on when their job is done. Treasure your crystals while they are with you, and let them bring you joy and happiness.

Types of crystal

Pointed: crystals with a point
Polished: rough crystals that have been abraded to create a polished surface
Rough: crystals in their natural, mined state
Rutilated: crystals, normally quartz, containing gold/red/black mineral strands
Striated: scratched, patterned, or grooved crystals
Terminated: crystals with a point
Tumbled: the same as polished, often placed in a large drum with grit to create smooth crystals

Silencing noisy neighbors with white moonstone

Polished, translucent

CRYSTAL FACTS

CRYSTAL TO USE: white moonstone, translucent

AVAILABILITY: commonly available

QUALITIES OF STONE: soothes stress, calms emotions and overreaction to problems

WHERE TO PLACE THE CRYSTAL: place by outside fence or internal wall in an apartment

You may be amazed at what a crystal can do to help you, even in the most intractable of situations. If noisy neighbors develop selective deafness whenever you ask for peace and quiet, try using a white moonstone, whose very name seems to suggest tranquility.

Moonstone is sacred in India because it is associated with the Third eye chakra, which relates to inner vision and the ability to take charge of your life. A symbol of love and confidence, moonstone will spark your intuition, helping you to find creative ways to solve potentially insurmountable problems. These qualities can inspire you to take a new view on an old or long-running dispute with a neighbor, breaking the cycle of annoyance and intolerance that has become established.

Crystal cure

Hold a white moonstone in your hand for several minutes and ask it to silence unwanted noise and disturbance. Place the stone outside, next to your neighbor's boundary; let it rest on the ledge of a fence or tuck it in a crevice in the mortar of a wall. If you are in an apartment, place the crystal on the floor next to the offending wall where it will not be disturbed.

Try this moonlight ritual to give your wish for peace more power. Wait until dark when the moon is in the sky, and pick a day when the moon is waning—the time between a full moon and a new moon, which symbolizes natural endings. Hold the stone as you look up at the moon in the night sky and simply ask for help. Repeat three times.

Trust in the stone's power. Within a few days, see how intrusive noise lessens and serenity takes its place.

ALTERNATIVE PROBLEM-SOLVING CRYSTALS TO USE

Sugilite: brings about compromise in difficult situations

Snowflake obsidian: a calming stone that can release negative thinking

Chrysoprase: a soothing stone that encourages positive solutions

Protecting your boundaries with agate

Agate is a brilliant crystal to use whenever you need a security guard for your home. Whether you call upon agate's powers of protection to deter unwanted visitors or intrusive neighbors, this crystal is renowned for keeping boundaries intact. It is a particularly grounding stone, bringing a sense of security and sanctuary.

Some traditions believed that agate made a person invisible to others. You can harness this gift by using the stone to help you go about your business with discretion, and without feeling constantly observed or overlooked by neighbors. Agate is therefore a great antidote to the "goldfish bowl" syndrome of many modern homes, and will help you any time you need privacy.

Crystal cure

To make you feel secure in the area surrounding your home, you need to bury a handful of small agate crystals on each side of your gate or driveway, and then bury one at each corner of the boundary of your garden or yard. This will literally activate the grounding quality of the stone. As you place the agates in the earth, ask the stones to help solve your problem and give you the peace and safety you desire in your space. Let the crystals do their work, and notice how happy you feel as you walk through your space as you sense the protective shield the agates have cast around the perimeter of your property.

Rough

CRYSTAL FACTS

CRYSTAL TO USE: agate (clear/milky white, gray, blue, green, pink, or brown); use small pieces

AVAILABILITY: commonly available

QUALITIES OF STONE: very grounding stone that creates a feeling of safety and security. Harmonizes yin and yang: the positive and negative forces of the universe

WHERE TO PLACE THE CRYSTAL: on either side of the gate and at boundary corners

ALTERNATIVE PROTECTIVE CRYSTALS TO USE

Hematite: a grounding and protective stone that dispels negativity

Jet: protects against violence, alleviates fears

Smoky quartz: neutralizes negative energy, blocks geopathic stress

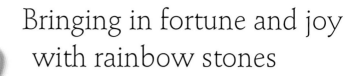

Bringing in fortune and joy with rainbow stones

Tubs of flowers that bloom year-round on each side of your front door are a welcoming presence for visitors. Sprinkling rainbow-colored tumbled stones over the tops of your flower pots creates a sense of peace, harmony, and joy around your entrance, and sets up a symbolic rainbow bridge of protection between your home and the spirit world. The color of the crystals—red, orange, yellow, green, turquoise blue, indigo, and violet—also links to the chakras, your spiritual energy centers, so you will benefit from an energy boost every time you enter your home.

CRYSTAL FACTS

CRYSTALS TO USE: choose two of the same tumbled stone from each rainbow color

Red: garnet, red jasper, ruby

Orange: carnelian, orange calcite

Yellow: amber, golden beryl, topaz

Green: aventurine, chrysoprase, malachite

Turquoise, blue, blue/green: aquamarine, celestite, turquoise

Indigo: lapis lazuli, sapphire, sodalite

Violet: amethyst, lavender (purple) jade, sugilite

QUALITIES OF STONES: using a selection of these crystals protects your home and brings purifying energy, joy and happiness, love and devotion, creativity and vitality, trust and peace, compassion, success, positive health and wellbeing, good fortune inside

WHERE TO PLACE THE CRYSTALS: place seven of the same stones in each flower tub on either side of the door

Crystal energizing

Choose your rainbow stones, place in a bowl, and leave them to energize in the sun for 24 hours (see also page 154). Wait for a showery, sunny day, when the crystals will be exposed to the powerful energy of a rainbow. Now hold the stones in your hands individually and ask each one to prevent any unwanted intrusions in your home. Ask them to surround you with their unique love and compassion. As you touch and gaze at each one, let their rainbow colors inspire you and your family with creativity and success at school and work, continued prosperity and health, and ask that they instill in you peace and hope for the future. Now scatter your seven stones evenly over the top of each pot and leave them to do their work.

Creating a party atmosphere for alfresco dining with red calcite

An opaque, soft stone, red calcite is an effective energizer. It has the ability to cleanse the environment of any unpleasant feelings, as well as injecting an appealing vitality into the atmosphere. It is the perfect stone to use for a picnic, barbecue, or alfresco dinner party because it links to the stimulating element of Fire, and projects the heat of the sun. Your guests will find themselves feeling happy and sociable as they respond to its warm, red, enigmatic vibrations.

Rough red calcite

Crystal energizing

Place the crystal in the middle of a designated dining table and watch how your friends mingle as they are drawn to stand around it happily sipping their aperitifs. The joy and happiness that emanate from the crystal are infectious, enlivening everyone within its radiance. To increase the buzz and to keep people staying for a while, scatter some chips of natural quartz, a great energizer, around the edges of the barbecue or picnic area. String some small, pretty, white lights along the ground where you have placed the crystals, as they are also associated with the Fire element and will lift the energetic vibrations.

CRYSTAL FACTS

CRYSTALS TO USE: red calcite: translucent, may be banded (sometimes treated with acid to increase color); small pieces of rough or tumbled quartz

AVAILABILITY: commonly available

QUALITIES OF STONES: red calcite: cleanses negative vibrations from the environment, increases energy and vitality for a party, creates a serene and joyful atmosphere; **natural quartz chips:** lift energy, bring a sparkling ambience

WHERE TO PLACE THE CRYSTALS: place red calcite on table. Scatter natural quartz chips around the perimeter of your dining area—your yard, garden, or deck

Polished quartz

Shielding your entrance with hematite

Rough

CRYSTAL FACTS

CRYSTAL TO USE: hematite (metallic silver/gray, red/brown when rough), also known as volcano spit; shiny appearance when polished, or use hematite chips

AVAILABILITY: commonly available

QUALITIES OF STONE: dissolves negativity, protects and prevents bad energies entering the home

WHERE TO PLACE THE CRYSTAL: by your outside doormat, or under the mat

Polished

In its rough, natural state, hematite is a reddish brown color. The crystal contains iron oxide and, because iron was associated with Mars, the Roman god of war, legend has it that Roman soldiers pressed the stone to their bodies for protection before battle. An environmentally grounding and supportive crystal, hematite, when polished, is metallic silvery gray, and produces such a high sheen that in the past it was used as a mirror, in much the same way as obsidian (see page 14).

Hematite's mirror effect can deflect the unpleasant attitudes of unwanted visitors at your front door. Although this area may feel good generally, people who unsuccessfully sell you goods or disgruntled visitors can all deplete the positivity of your entrance. Placing hematite by the front door can smooth the flow of energy. A powerful protector, the stone builds a healing shield around the entrance. This shield connects to the earth's beneficial properties, neutralizing any bad energy that people bring with them, so that even those who come to the door feeling upset go away happy.

Crystal cure

Place a hematite crystal outside the door by the doormat, or in an apartment you may prefer to scatter some hematite chips under the mat. Hold them and ask that they protect your entrance and heal all the people that call there. Trust in their curative powers.

ALTERNATIVE PROTECTIVE CRYSTALS TO USE

Selenite: creates a peaceful space, keeps out bad influences

Obsidian: very protective, shields negative forces

Polished

CRYSTAL FACTS

CRYSTAL TO USE: green jade, translucent (jadeite) or creamy (nephrite)

AVAILABILITY: generally available but can be rare; nephrite is more easily available

QUALITIES OF STONE: encourages peace and unconditional love, protects and nurtures, creates harmony, brings good luck

WHERE TO PLACE THE CRYSTAL: stick next to mail box, or put inside

Increasing luck and good fortune with green jade

Jade is a stone of prosperity and luck that will draw money and good things into your life, and so is perfect for placing by your mailbox. Two types of this beneficial crystal are available: the creamy nephrite is the "older" dark leafy-green jade, which was carved into many treasured pieces in ancient China from as early as 2950 BCE, while the "newer" translucent, vivid green jadeite originated in Burma in the 13th century. As jadeite took over in popularity from nephrite in China, it was worshipped for its life-extending and erotic properties.

Jade bestows tranquility and wisdom, transmitting a sense of wellbeing and friendship that welcomes people into your home. It is also protective, so will act as a deterrent to burglars or unsavory visitors.

Crystal energizing

To bring good fortune and abundance into your home, take hold of your jade crystal and tune in to its lucky vibrations. Using reusable adhesive putty, stick the crystal to the side of your letterbox or mailbox (inside the front door) or if you have an outside mailbox, place it inside. Let this joyous stone protect you, and ask it to attract success and many lucky opportunities.

Harmonizing the hallway with magical obsidian

Formed from volcanic lava, obsidian was used by the Aztecs as the equivalent of flint, to make knives and arrowheads. When finely polished it is deeply reflective, and the stone's magical reputation is perhaps due to its mirrorlike qualities; Dr. Jon Dee, spiritual adviser to Queen Elizabeth I, prized an Aztec "magic mirror" of obsidian for scrying, or future-gazing. As everyone who lives with you or visits can bring the mixed emotions of their day to your door, you can use this ancient stone as a symbolic mirror to deflect incoming frustrations and upsets.

Rough

CRYSTAL FACTS

CRYSTAL TO USE: black obsidian, opaque, shiny, similar to glass, sometimes tumbled

AVAILABILITY: commonly available

QUALITIES OF STONE: a very grounding stone that repels or transforms negativity, blocks geopathic stress, encourages optimism for the future

WHERE TO PLACE THE CRYSTAL: on hall table, to the side of the front door

Crystal cure

Place a black obsidian crystal, either tumbled or raw, in your hallway—the best position is on a small table or on a corner shelf by the front door. Bear in mind that poor lighting and clutter can inhibit your crystal's abilities, so keep your hall's surfaces clear and the whole space bright. Hold this crystal tightly and ask it to do its work for you, and soon this grounding stone will neutralize any negativity that has been brought in, and restore a more harmonious ambience.

ALTERNATIVE HARMONIZING CRYSTALS TO USE

Citrine: brings in the feeling of sunlight, brightening dull areas

Clear topaz: helps to clear stagnant or stuck energy

Brown jasper: brings stability and balance; relieves environmental stress

Encouraging good energy flow on stairs with natural quartz

Versatile natural quartz can increase energy or transmute any negative influences, and is easily programmed to suit your needs. This crystal can transmit electrical energy under mechanical pressure, creating the piezoelectric effect. To see this in action, rub the flat sides of two quartz crystals together in a darkened room and see how the friction makes the stones light up. You can also "lighten up" your home by placing slivers of natural quartz on the stair treads or under banisters to create a vibrant pathway between floors, enlivening the energy flow from the downstairs rooms.

Crystal cure

If you sense the energy in your home is dull and lacking in vibrancy due to building work or if you have cleared out a lot of clutter, you can improve the flow of energy between floors by gluing or fixing $1/2$in (12mm) pieces of rough or polished quartz to the sides of the stair treads. Mount one each side to the bottom tread, one each side to the top, and then place one each side of a tread in between. Alternatively, glue two slivers in the same places but under the banister rail. These crystals are wonderful energizers and will take the energy frequency higher, which will then impact on you and your family, making you feel happier and more content in your home.

Polished

CRYSTAL FACTS

CRYSTAL TO USE: six $1/2$in (12mm) small quartz pieces, polished or rough

AVAILABILITY: commonly available

QUALITIES OF STONE: amplifies energy, regulates energy flow

WHERE TO PLACE THE CRYSTAL: glue crystals to the side of four stair treads, equally spaced up the stairs, or stick to the underside of the banisters

Polished

Purifying house energies with rose quartz

In chakra healing, rose quartz is traditionally used to purify the heart, the place of deep emotion and, in some ancient cultures, the soul. Associated with love, this sensitive stone dispels the bad atmosphere that most arguments bring, and clears the air after an illness, children's tantrums, or a string of minor domestic problems. Pure and uplifting, rose quartz can be used to clear residual negativity and bring happy harmony to your home.

Polished

CRYSTAL FACTS

CRYSTAL TO USE: rose quartz (pink), translucent, use a medium-size raw chunk

AVAILABILITY: commonly available

QUALITIES OF STONE: removes negative energy, replacing it with loving vibrations

WHERE TO PLACE THE CRYSTAL: make a crystal essence by soaking the stone in mineral water

Crystal cure

For an immediate energy lift in your home, and to restore its loving vibrations after an argument or another energy-depleting incident, you can spray all the rooms with a rose quartz essence.

Crystal essences are often compared to flower essences as an energetic imprint of the crystal is believed to be left in the water in which it is soaked. They are simple to make. Rinse your rose quartz crystal under running water, then place in a glass container or jar. Fill the container with still mineral water until the stone is covered. Cover the container and place on a table or windowsill where it is bathed in sunlight. Ideally leave for 1–12 hours: the longer you leave it the stronger the essence will be. Pour off the liquid in to a mister bottle. Hold the bottle in your hands and ask the essence to use its soothing and healing vibrations to remove any unhappiness in your home. Hold this thought in your head as you spray in each room, moving around clockwise from the doorway. Use regularly after upsets or other disruptions.

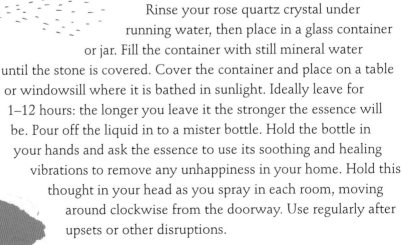

Promoting harmony with a water fountain and stones

A mini water fountain enhanced with crystals will bring harmony and balance to your living room. The stones, which individually possess the gifts of love, peace, and compassion that we want to attract into our lives, collectively create a sacred object—the font. "Fountain" is derived from the Old French word *fontaine* and the Latin *fontana*, meaning font, indicating baptism and purification by water. A crystal water fountain purifies negativity, instilling good energy flow and feelings of calm and relaxation. The trickling water also emits negative ions, giving off a positive, stimulating vibe.

Crystal energizing

Buy the polished crystals detailed below, searching out colors and shapes that most appeal to you. Place this chosen assortment of stones in the pebbles so that their emanations soothe, foster tranquility and purity, and induce a balanced and harmonious atmosphere.

Position the fountain on a dining table, a prominent shelf, or to give your Wealth corner a boost, in the southeast corner of the living room. Notice how people are drawn toward this inspiring feature as soon as they enter the room.

CRYSTAL FACTS

CRYSTALS TO USE: polished tiger's eye, brown jasper, carnelian, jade or aventurine (green), turquoise or sodalite (blue) plus a pump-operated water fountain with pebbles

AVAILABILITY: commonly available

QUALITIES OF STONES: using this selection of stones creates serenity, peace, stability, balance, harmony, friendship, empathy, calmness, and a passion for life

WHERE TO PLACE THE CRYSTALS: in the water fountain on a table or shelf, or in the southeast of the living room

Balancing emotions with a crystal tree

A crystal tree in your living room can soothe the fluctuating emotions of your family. The three crystals on the tree—sodalite, amethyst, and rose quartz—have the special qualities of peace, love, and tranquility that all of us in our stressed, modern lives crave. Placing these stones on a tree evokes a grounded feeling, of putting down deep roots into Mother Earth: trees protect and reassure. The ancient Greeks talked to trees, believing they contained all the wisdom of the gods. Just looking at this pretty tree will bring a sense of hope and optimism; destructive moods such as irritability or anger have no place around this evocative symbol.

Crystal cure

Place your tree on a prominent shelf or on a side table where it catches people's attention. Or, place it in the east to get the benefit of the inherent family and good health energies that exist there. Notice how the interaction of your family improves around this tree, and how a visitor's demeanor softens as they are influenced by the pacifying and spiritual elements of the crystals.

CRYSTAL FACTS

CRYSTALS TO USE: sodalite, amethyst, and rose quartz tree or individual trees of these crystals

AVAILABILITY: commonly available

QUALITIES OF STONES: sodalite: stills and cleanses the mind, increases relaxation, releases stress, boosts self-esteem; **amethyst:** dispels anger and anxiety, balances emotions, increases intuition, calms or stimulates as appropriate, brings tranquility and peace, aids spirituality and meditation; **rose quartz:** attracts love, peace, happiness, promotes self-love, heals the emotions, removes negative energy, strengthens empathy and sensitivity

WHERE TO PLACE THE CRYSTALS: living room shelf or side table and/or in the east of the room

Dowsing for geopathic stress and neutralizing it with amethyst

Natural quartz and amethyst are both piezoelectric, which means that they have a positive and negative polarity and can emit electromagnetic energy. These highly sensitive stones can be used in dowsing to identify and neutralize negative earth energies, or geopathic stress, which can cause lethargy and general tiredness.

The human body adapts to normal earth energies (or radiation waves) that come up through the ground. Geopathic stress occurs when these energies become distorted, often due to the presence of a stream, tunnel, or old mine under your property. Another cause of energetic discomfort may be ley lines—the strong energies that run along a fault or strata—particularly if your home sits on a ley-line junction, where two intersect.

Polished

CRYSTAL FACTS

CRYSTAL TO USE: natural quartz pendulum; 2 large or several small pieces of amethyst

AVAILABILITY: commonly available

QUALITIES OF STONE: amethyst: a powerful protective stone that blocks geopathic stress or negative environmental energies

WHERE TO PLACE THE CRYSTAL: in the places where negative energy registers

Crystal cure

To find if you have any negative energy areas in your living room you need to dowse for them. Take your natural quartz pendulum and ask it to indicate which is the answer "yes": it normally spins in a clockwise direction. Then ask for "no": it normally spins counterclockwise, but these can be reversed. Then walk around the room, stopping at different points, and ask the pendulum, "Are there are any negative earth energies here that are affecting my health?" Note down any areas where it swings positively. Place two large pieces of amethyst in the affected areas, or place several small pieces under the carpet, asking for their help in neutralizing the negative vibrations that are adversely affecting your health.

ALTERNATIVE PROTECTIVE CRYSTALS TO USE

Rose quartz: soothes away harsh energy

Smoky quartz: gently neutralizes unhealthy earth vibrations

Obsidian: creates a shield against negative energy

Reviving houseplants with green tourmaline

Also known as verdelite, green tourmaline is associated with the Heart chakra, or love center, and it is renowned as a healing stone. Associated with Venus and the element of Earth, this crystal also represents fertility, which is why you can use it to revive your houseplants and encourage their healthy growth.

Houseplants are wonderful energizers in a living room as they lift the atmosphere and help to increase the oxygen content, and many of them improve humidity, filter the air, and cleanse it of pollutants such as formaldehyde, which is often present in new carpets and some furniture. So if you have any houseplants that are not growing well or look sickly, it is essential to give them some care to help them thrive again and keep the living room's ambience positive and vibrant.

Polished

CRYSTAL FACTS

CRYSTAL TO USE: green tourmaline, shiny, opaque, long or hexagon stone

AVAILABILITY: easily available from specialist stores

QUALITIES OF STONE: wonderful healer; brings balance and aids growth

WHERE TO PLACE THE CRYSTAL: in the soil of the plant pot

Crystal cure

If you have a plant (or several) that are in need of some love and attention, remove any dead leaves or flowers and trim back any dead stalks. Now take your green tourmaline and hold it in your hands for a few minutes. Tune into its emanations and ask for its loving help to make your plant healthy and vital again.

Place the stone on the soil by the plant stem, and see how in a few weeks your plant starts to come back to life. To aid growth leave the crystal in the pot for a while, but cleanse it regularly (see pages 149–153).

ALTERNATIVE HEALTH-GIVING CRYSTALS TO USE

Aventurine: a balancing stone that can regulate growth

Natural quartz: an energizer that increases growth and expansion

Turquoise: helps plants to recover from disease or infestation

Prolonging cut flowers with quartz crystal

Like green tourmaline (see opposite) you can also use quartz and smoky quartz to heal and sustain plants. A natural energizer, quartz can purify water, so it is the perfect choice for prolonging the life of cut flowers, which soon lose their life force.

Crystal cure

Use quartz crystals with a point or terminated end rather than a cluster, because the point will channel focused energy toward the flower stems and help them stay vital. Hold the crystal in your hands for a few minutes and ask for its help in extending the life of your beautiful flowers, then let it sink gently into the vase's water. Alternatively, if you have a large vase of flowers, dedicate three pointed crystals (see page 155) and then place them, with their points inward, in different positions facing the vase. Alternatively, use a quartz crystal or smoky quartz wand (see below, right). In this way the flowers will receive an amplified energy force to keep them looking fresh and lovely for longer.

CRYSTAL FACTS

CRYSTAL TO USE: quartz or smoky quartz pointed (terminator) crystals and/or wands

AVAILABILITY: commonly available

QUALITIES OF STONE: energy amplifier, powerful healer, also cleanses water

WHERE TO PLACE THE CRYSTAL: in the vase, or put several around the vase

Smoky quartz wand

Getting sociable with five-element crystals

CRYSTAL FACTS

CRYSTALS TO USE: choose at least one crystal from each of these element groups:

Water crystals (blue, purple, black): amethyst, aquamarine, jet

Earth crystals (yellow and brown): citrine, tiger's eye

Metal crystals (white): opal, selenite, snow quartz

Wood crystals (green): jade, moss agate

Fire crystals (red, pink): red calcite, red jasper, rose quartz

QUALITIES OF STONES: using a selection of these crystals energizes, cleanses, and protects the atmosphere, encouraging peace, love, and spontaneity, good communication, harmony, and balance.

WHERE TO PLACE THE CRYSTALS: on a coffee table, side table, or shelf in the east of the living room. Don't place on a windowsill as sunshine can overstimulate them.

In feng shui—the art of furniture placement and good energy flow—the five Chinese elements of Water, Earth, Fire, Wood, and Metal work together to produce harmony in a space. By choosing crystals from each of the element groups and displaying them together, you create a symbol of perfect balance and happiness. By placing your bowl in the east of the living room, you activate the properties of that sector—in feng shui, the east represents harmonious relationships with family and friends.

Crystal energizing

A bowl of five-element crystals creates a balanced ambience in a room that needs a relaxed yet convivial atmosphere. As well as providing an aesthetic talking point, your chosen crystals will create a scintillating buzz, inspiring stimulating conversation with friends and plenty of joy and laughter.

Buy both natural clusters and polished crystals that look good together, and display in a clear glass bowl so that you can see them from every angle. Remember to cleanse the stones every few weeks (see pages 149–153) to keep their energies vibrant.

Attracting prosperity and success with citrine, rose quartz, and aventurine

The combination of citrine, aventurine, and rose quartz can attract the money and success you want in your life. Aventurine is an all-round good luck stone, and in ancient magical rites was used to heighten perception and intelligence (after all, you need your wits about you as you wheel and deal your way to wealth!). Along with its wealth-creating properties, citrine fights the fear that holds you back, so you create the prosperous future that you desire. Rose quartz instills a loving atmosphere receptive to success, balancing existing yin and yang energies.

Crystal energizing

In feng shui, the southeast represents your corner of wealth and prosperity. To boost the energy in this area of your living room, place citrine, rose quartz, and aventurine crystals in the southeast on a table or shelf. The combined qualities of these crystals raise the vibrations in this area to attract the prosperity and success you want.

A crystal wishing spell

Write down your wish on a piece of paper. Hold it for a moment, meditating on your desire. Fold and place under the crystals so that positive energies go into your wish and help make it come true.

CRYSTAL FACTS

CRYSTALS TO USE: citrine (yellow), commonly a geode or cluster; rose quartz (pink), natural or polished; aventurine (green), opaque with shiny particles, usually tumbled

QUALITIES OF STONES: this trinity of stones brings the following benefits: **citrine:** brings energy, inspiring you to manifest and create wealth and success, also has a reputation as a "psychic" stone, helping you hear your intuition; **rose quartz:** evokes self-trust, self-love, and self-worth; **aventurine:** associated with prosperity, it has been known as a gambler's talisman, also enhances creativity

WHERE TO PLACE THE CRYSTALS: in the southeast corner of your living room

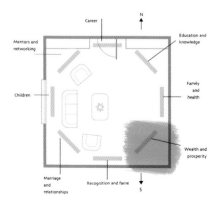

Display rose quartz, citrine, and aventurine in the southeast of your living room.

Check the orientation of the room with a compass and mark all the directions on a room plan.

Reducing TV electromagnetic stress with lepidolite

Lepidolite is a purplish fragile mineral that is a type of mica, rich in the silvery metal lithium. A very calming crystal, it can soothe an overstressed nervous system. The rough mica form of the crystal has greatly amplified properties that absorb any negative energies in a room, and its high vibratory rate also neutralizes artificial electro-magnetic fields (EMFs) generated by televisions and other electrical equipment in the living room. Our bodies are used to the natural electromagnetic emissions that come up through the earth's surface, although they can be affected by distorted energy (see page 19). However, we have not adjusted to artificial EMFs, which can upset our immune systems because of the excessive electrical radiation that makes us more vulnerable to illness.

Rough

CRYSTAL FACTS

CRYSTAL TO USE: lepidolite (lavender, but may be pink), shiny surfaced, grainy stone. The rough (mica) form amplifies its properties.

AVAILABILITY: commonly available

QUALITIES OF STONE: can clear or absorb electromagnetic pollution; dispels negativity

WHERE TO PLACE THE CRYSTAL: by side of your television, on the TV cabinet, or stick to shelf

Crystal cure

Children in particular can often sit

too close to televisions, so encourage them to move back (as you should do) to at least 6–10ft (1.8–3m) from the set as the EMF reduces the farther away you sit. To help protect you from this radiation, take a lepidolite crystal in your hands for a few minutes and ask it to use its cleansing abilities to reduce the harmful EMFs emitted from your television. Now place it next to the set or, with reusable adhesive putty, stick it to the TV cabinet or the shelf it sits on. Over the next few days, observe how you feel more grounded and energized as the crystal acts to purify your space.

ALTERNATIVE EMF-REDUCING CRYSTALS TO USE

Fluorite: highly protective, dispels electromagnetic stress (right: blue purple fluorite)

Kunzite: shields you from unwanted energies, disperses negative forces

Deflecting negative chi with a lead-faceted crystal

Lead-faceted crystals, made from glass, are wonderful energizers to have in your living room. They are not as powerful as natural quartz, but amplify and lift the energy, or chi, that filters through the window, making the atmosphere come alive. A round (spherical), multifaceted crystal is the most holistic one to hang, and is regularly used by feng shui consultants. As the crystal spins in front of the window it refracts the sunlight through the cut-glass ball, making prisms of color and letting the full spectrum of rainbow colors flow into the room. These colors are also linked to the chakras (spiritual energy centers) so basically the world is your oyster—you are bringing the maximum potential into the room. Hanging in the window, the crystal moves gently in the air currents, stirring up the energy flow in the room so it feels fresh and bright, or newly spring-cleaned.

Spherical lead-faceted
hanging crystal

CRYSTAL FACTS

CRYSTAL TO USE: lead-faceted, spherical hanging crystal, 1in (25mm) for average-size room; 2in (50mm) for a large room

AVAILABILITY: commonly available

QUALITIES OF STONE: amplifies energy, creates a vibrant and happy atmosphere

WHERE TO PLACE THE CRYSTAL: hang it from the top of a window frame or the ceiling

Lead-faceted
hanging crystal

Crystal cure

The best place to display this crystal is toward the top of the window. Position it so that it hangs in the middle of a pane of glass, suspended by a pin or nail from the wood above, or possibly the ceiling. Before you hang the crystal, hold it in your hands briefly and ask it to bring wonderful energy and color into your room. Notice how the energetics of the room take a step upward over the next week or so as the crystal starts to do its sparkling work. Cleanse weekly by dipping in spring water and leaving to dry in the sun.

Promoting happy relationships with amethyst and citrine

Cut and
polished
citrine

In feng shui, different combinations of crystals can strengthen the energetic forces in your aspirational areas. The pairing of amethyst and citrine lifts the harmonics of your marriage and relationship space in the southwest of your living room, raising the love vibes here and increasing your chances of meeting a new partner or strengthening an existing liaison. Amethyst is a supreme healing crystal that lets you get in touch with your feelings. Pure and true love comes out of this stone, making lovers want to exchange the crystal in the shape of a heart to show how committed they are. Citrine has a special affinity with amethyst, as it can be formed by heat-treating amethyst to achieve the yellowy citrine color and vibration. A stone of prosperity, citrine fills you with joy and makes you feel good about yourself. Meditating with citrine increases your spiritual connection, giving you more mental clarity about how to progress with your relationship or find that desired new partner.

CRYSTAL FACTS

CRYSTALS TO USE: amethyst cluster (violet/purple), transparent; faceted or smooth tumbled citrine, or citrine cluster (golden, yellow, yellow/brown)

AVAILABILITY: commonly available

QUALITIES OF STONES: these two crystals bring the following benefits: **amethyst:** promotes love, spiritual wisdom, and intuition. It enhances memory and improves motivation. The crystal lends courage to the wearer and is a protective amulet for travelers; **citrine:** a crystal that encourages happiness and generosity, it imparts joy in love and raises self-esteem and self-belief, while also attracting money into your life. Placed under the pillow it ensures a goodnight's sleep.

WHERE TO PLACE THE CRYSTALS: in the southwest of the living room

Crystal energizing

Display chunks of these crystals together on a shelf or in the southwest of your living room and see how they raise the energetics, improving your relationship luck. Keep them away from too much sun as they may fade, particularly dark amethyst. Putting them with red candles, happy partnership pictures or photographs and a paired statue says to the world that you want a current, or desired, relation-ship to work.

Amethyst cluster

Aiding sleep with hematite

Hematite is an extremely grounding crystal, inducing feelings of safety and comfort. It has the reputed ability to help the regeneration of body tissue—one of the prime purposes of sleep—which may explain the connection between hematite and sleeping well.

The ancient Egyptians used hematite to quell hysteria and anxiety, which often cause sleep disturbance; during difficult emotional times, or when the mind and body are overactive, insomnia may strike. If you regularly suffer from disrupted sleep, you will often feel fatigued and irritable throughout the day. Using hematite promotes deep, healing sleep and will calm a grasshopper mind, allowing you to recharge at every level.

Polished

CRYSTAL FACTS

CRYSTAL TO USE: hematite (metallic silver/gray) tumbled and polished

AVAILABILITY: commonly available

QUALITIES OF STONE: induces a deep restful sleep, dissolves negativity and protects the soul

WHERE TO PLACE THE CRYSTAL: under the pillow

Crystal cure

Use a tumbled hematite crystal and experience its grounding and revitalizing properties. Choose a stone that you know wants to help you and feels pleasing to you when you turn it over in your hand. Go into your bedroom and sit on the bed, holding your crystal. Light a candle and sit with your eyes closed, tuning in to the stone's nurturing energies. When you feel ready, ask for better sleep and help in resolving any crisis you may be experiencing. Before bed, place the crystal under your pillow, where your head rests.

ALTERNATIVE SLEEP-INDUCING CRYSTALS TO USE

Chrysoprase: induces peaceful and relaxing sleep, unlocks blocked emotions

Aventurine: promotes emotional tranquility and positive attitudes

Golden topaz: recharges the spirit and relieves nervous exhaustion

Boosting passion with ruby

A stone of love, ruby is believed to open up the Heart chakra—the heart's spiritual energy center—to joy and bliss. In ancient Egypt the stone was held in high regard, and anyone who acquired the ruby was thought to gain beauty and good fortune. In Hindu culture, it was given the name the "king of precious stones," because of its magnificence. Legend says that an everlasting flame burned in the jewel, which is probably why today its fiery qualities are believed to instill passion and sexual allure into the person wearing it. This is the ideal stone to bring some passion back into your love life, as the dynamism of this crystal will charge up your enthusiasm for making love and increase your sex appeal.

Rough

CRYSTAL FACTS

CRYSTAL TO USE: ruby (red), uncut, opaque

AVAILABILITY: commonly available

QUALITIES OF STONE: charges up passion, attracts some sexual activity, stimulates the Heart chakra, and increases potency

WHERE TO PLACE THE CRYSTAL: hold to heart, then place on your bedside table

Crystal energizing

Keep your ruby safe in a drawer and bring it out only when you want to feel sensual with your partner; otherwise, the stone may emit energy that is intense and stimulating, and not conducive to sleep and relaxation. To connect with your crystal, hold it right next to your heart for a few minutes, close your eyes, and ask it to restore any lost or waning passion and romantic feelings in your life. Now place the crystal on the bedside cabinet or nightstand and go to bed, knowing that it will lift the loving vibrations between you and your partner.

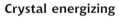

ALTERNATIVE PASSION-INDUCING CRYSTALS TO USE

Carnelian: restores vitality, overcomes reserve, increases fertility

Garnet: revitalizes energy, bringing passion and sexual potency

Smoky quartz: enhances sexual fervor, helps acceptance of body

Releasing worries at night with sodalite

This deep-blue crystal, colored like the sky at twilight, can clear your mind of upset, bringing objectivity and solutions to problems that may be keeping you awake at night. If you regularly go to bed plagued by all the day's problems, or you have worked late into the evening to try to resolve financial or family concerns, your brain will not rest and peaceful sleep may elude you.

Sodalite is associated with insight and wisdom—this "true blue" stone, associated with the Third eye chakra of inner wisdom, can help you discover the truth behind a troubling situation. It is also thought to help you remember your dreams, which can give you valuable insight into the type of problems you are experiencing.

Polished heart

CRYSTAL FACTS

CRYSTAL TO USE: sodalite, dark blue, blue/white variegated stone

AVAILABILITY: commonly available

QUALITIES OF STONE: helps to eliminate mental confusion, calms and clears mind, and brings new perceptions, alleviates fear

WHERE TO PLACE THE CRYSTAL: hold to forehead, then leave on bedside table

Crystal cure

To prepare for better sleep, it is always best to release worries or alleviate them before going to bed. Sit on your bed, close your eyes and breathe deeply, then hold your crystal to your Third eye chakra in the middle of your forehead for about five minutes, focusing on your problems, and let the crystal do its work to calm your mind. When you feel relaxed, place the crystal on your bedside cabinet or nightstand and lay down to sleep. Remember to cleanse your stone regularly (see pages 149–153).

ALTERNATIVE WORRY-RELEASING CRYSTALS TO USE

Onyx: reduces overwhelming worries and fears

Azurite (or azurite with malachite): clears worries, bringing solutions

Apophyllite: calms, and ameliorates negative thought patterns

Encouraging good study with gold calcite

Gold calcite is an ideal mind-boosting crystal. Associated with mental empowerment, it may amplify your child's efforts toward academic success. Its legendary powers of focus and concentration may be due to the reputation of one of its cousins, optical calcite, which visually duplicates whatever it touches: placed over a symbol such as a star, it will literally appear double. Gold calcite is also associated with creativity, so it will stimulate and support your child in their artistic pursuits and encourage a creative approach to projects.

Rough

CRYSTAL FACTS

CRYSTAL TO USE: gold calcite, translucent, waxy, sometimes tumbled

AVAILABILITY: commonly available

QUALITIES OF STONE: stimulates insight, boosts memory, helps mind retain important information

WHERE TO PLACE THE CRYSTAL: on child's desk

Crystal energizing

To focus your child on their studies at home, place a gold calcite crystal on his desk close to where he reads and writes. This stone helps keep him alert mentally, giving him extra motivation and increasing his memory skills. If he is struggling with a difficult task, get him to hold the crystal for a while and ask for its help to solve his homework problems.

In feng shui, the education and knowledge sector is located in the northeast of a room, so, ideally, place your child's desk here so that he can benefit from the supportive education and knowledge energies. If this is not possible, place the gold calcite in the northeast sector of his desk so that he can still benefit from the good energies.

ALTERNATIVE STUDY CRYSTALS TO USE

Blue chalcedony: stimulates learning skills, promotes mental flexibility

Fluorite: encourages quick thinking, helps to assimilate information (right: purple fluorite)

Howlite: increases memory and engenders a desire for knowledge

Balancing children's energies with pink or blue crystals

Traditionally, blue clothes were bought for baby boys and pink for girls. It is not known how this tradition originated, but it does link in with feng shui principles. In feng shui, boys (or men) are considered to be yang people. Yang is associated with positive actions, the sun, heaven, vigor, light, fire, and warmth. Girls (or women) are yin people and are thought to be more passive, linked to darkness, the earth, negativity, cold, the moon, stillness, and water. To thrive, children need a balance of both these forces. To calm overly energetic children, paint their rooms in blue or green, but if energizing is needed, decorate the room in pinks and oranges. Positioning some pink and blue crystals on the bedside cabinet or nightstand will also harmonize these energies.

Crystal energizing

To balance too much yin, choose one of the pink crystals below for some yang (warm) energy to develop a child's passion for life, their self-expression, willpower and energy, and empathy and sensitivity. To balance too much yang, choose a blue stone for some yin (cool) energy to quieten a child's mind, bring inner strength for change, calm mental confusion, and balance the nervous system. Let your child choose the crystal with you. They may feel a slight pulsating sensation as they find the "right" one. Explain how it can help to calm or energize, and place the crystal by their bed so that its embracing and energies are with them all the time.

Rough kunzite

Rough rose quartz

Rough sodalite

Rough turquoise

CRYSTAL FACTS

CRYSTALS TO CHOOSE FROM:

Pink: rhodochrosite, kunzite (above), rose quartz (above)

Blue: sodalite (right), aquamarine, chrysocolla, turquoise (right)

AVAILABILITY: commonly available

QUALITIES OF STONES: pink: increases energetic vibrations and motivation; blue: calms energies, cleansing the body and quietening the mind

WHERE TO PLACE THE CRYSTALS: on bedside cabinet or nightstand

Stimulating creativity with quartz

Polished quartz

Natural quartz is perfect for stimulating creativity and focus in a child's room. You can bring in this energy in the form of rough quartz or polished crystal birds or animals, such as a quartz owl or cat, which are easy to find, or go for rough or polished pieces of rutilated quartz. With pretty golden or coppery fibers, rutilated quartz has a slightly different energy from that of clear quartz—it is associated with stirring the spirit, and can help heighten the natural creativity that is so free-flowing in a child.

As children grow up, the artistic side of their personalities flourish; activities such as drawing, painting, or playing a musical instrument may appeal. With either art they can express the mixed emotions of their day and become immersed in the pleasure of a stimulating hobby. The special qualities of quartz crystal can support a budding talent, developing a sense of potential and skill in their chosen pursuit.

CRYSTAL FACTS

CRYSTAL TO USE: natural or polished clear quartz, and/or rutilated quartz (clear or milky with silver, gold, copper-colored, brown, red, or black strands); also known as angel hair

AVAILABILITY: commonly available

QUALITIES OF STONE: helps inspiration, magnifies positive energy, gives creative insight, focuses and directs the mind

WHERE TO PLACE THE CRYSTAL: place on table or on windowsill of play area

Crystal energizing

The play area of a bedroom is generally the place where children will lose themselves in drawing or practicing a favorite musical instrument. Screen off this stimulating area from the sleep space and place the quartz crystal on a work table or on a nearby windowsill. Let this stone release its energizing and inspiring aura so that it surrounds your child, increasing their concentration and flair.

Polished rutilated quartz

Alleviating nightmares with lepidolite

Rough

Lepidolite is a delicate mineral that is incredibly soothing, associated with easing many painful emotions such as anger, hate, irritability, or sadness. An alternative name is "peace stone," because the caring properties of the crystal take away tension and anxiety, which often create the vivid imagery of nightmares that many young children experience. Breathing problems from a cold or anxiety over school problems can trigger the nightmares.

CRYSTAL FACTS

CRYSTAL TO USE: lepidolite (lavender, may be pink), layered tone, can be shiny or grainy

AVAILABILITY: commonly available

QUALITIES OF STONE: calms sleep disturbances, reduces emotional fears, brings deep inner healing

WHERE TO PLACE THE CRYSTAL: on bedside cabinet or nightstand

Crystal cure

If your child is frightened to go to sleep because of recurring nightmares, take the lepidolite crystal in your hand and explain to your child how this comforting stone takes away their anxieties, and will soothe their mind when they are asleep; you can both make up a story about it, if you choose to. Let your child feel the crystal and connect with its gentle energies, then place it on their bedside cabinet or nightstand to let it form a worry-free zone around their bed. Leave the crystal there each night until the nightmares stop. Cleanse the crystal well to keep it vibrant (see pages 149–153).

ALTERNATIVE NIGHTMARE-RELIEVING CRYSTALS TO USE

Amethyst: dispels fear and anxiety, soothes an overactive mind

Purple fluorite: removes and purifies negative energies

Lapis lazuli: releases stress and brings deep serenity

Restoring energy with jade in the bath

Polished egg

Known in ancient China as the "stone of heaven," jade has adorned temples, promoted longevity, and defended the Mayans and Maoris, who had it hewn into arrowheads and axes. Yet beneath its literally hard exterior jade has a softer side, as it is a stone associated with healing and love. The Chinese crushed it to a powder for ingestion as a remedy, and it is the crystal of Kuan Yin, the Buddhist Madonna and goddess of compassion. Bathing with jade restores depleted energy, reenergizes the nervous system, and brings inner peace.

CRYSTAL FACTS

CRYSTAL TO USE: jade (green), opaque to translucent, often polished or tumbled

AVAILABILITY: commonly available

QUALITIES OF STONE: cleanses, restores emotional balance, disperses negative thoughts, gently energizes

WHERE TO PLACE THE CRYSTAL: in the bath or a footbath

Crystal energizing

Placing a crystal in the bathwater or in a footbath will bring the energy boost that your body is seeking. Fill your bath or a large bowl with warm water; if bathing, surround the tub with lit

candles to bring in some extra, positive energy. Hold your stone briefly and connect to its nurturing energies, asking it to help you let go of the stress of the day. Place it in the bath and leave for a few minutes, then step in. Feel the water embracing you and the soft vibrations of the stone revitalizing your physical body and energetic field. Relax in the bath for about 10 minutes. Afterward remove your stone, and thank it for its help.

ALTERNATIVE ENERGIZING CRYSTALS TO USE

Amazonite: reduces worries and fears, alleviates negative energy

Peridot: acts as tonic for body and mind, dispels stress

Onyx: lessens stress, promotes vigor and stamina

Lifting the atmosphere in the bathroom with citrine

Citrine is a lovely, generous, and beneficial stone that is believed to take its name from the French *citron,* for lemon, as many of the crystals have a bright, lemon color. It is a member of the quartz family, and because of its connection to the sun, it projects pleasure and optimism. Its warming and energizing qualities are perfect for the bathroom, where the atmosphere can be humid with a sluggish energetic flow. It also has the ability to transmute and dissolve negative energy, and because of this never needs cleansing. Often known as the merchant's stone, citrine attracts prosperity and abundance into your life with its happy and generous aura.

Crystal energizing

In the bathroom a lot of steam and condensation is generated, which can make the atmosphere feel rather heavy or oppressive. Placing a chunk of citrine on a bathroom shelf to sparkle in the sun, or by the bath, can reverse this sensation and brighten the ambience. Hold the stone in your hands and feel its vibrancy raising your self-esteem; it is a stone that always makes you feel good about yourself. Ask it to spread its natural enthusiasm into the room and to keep the atmosphere light and airy, then place it in position.

Cluster

CRYSTAL FACTS

CRYSTAL TO USE: citrine (yellow, yellow/brown), transparent, often a cluster

AVAILABILITY: natural citrine can be rare; citrine produced by heat-treating amethyst is commonly available

QUALITIES OF STONE: powerful cleansing stone, lifts and warms atmosphere, encourages mental clarity and optimism, heals any negativity

WHERE TO PLACE THE CRYSTAL: on a shelf or by the bath

Cut and polished

ALTERNATIVE ENERGIZING CRYSTALS TO USE

Carnelian: energizes a room and gives it increased vitality

Red jasper: gently stimulates energy, absorbs any negativity

Green fluorite: dissolves any negativity, cleanses, purifies, and helps re-energize the atmosphere

Polished

CRYSTAL FACTS

CRYSTAL TO USE: aquamarine, (green/blue), clear or opaque, can be faceted, although often tumbled

AVAILABILITY: commonly available

QUALITIES OF STONE: brings peace, surrounds and fills a room with feelings of love and inspiration, purifies and calms the atmosphere, encourages emotional balance

WHERE TO PLACE THE CRYSTAL: on the side of the bath, or on a shelf where you can see it while bathing

Harmonizing energies with aquamarine

Aquamarine is a semiprecious member of the beryl family. Its lovely greeny-blue, sparkly color instantly reminds you of the soothing waves of the sea. It was once believed to be the stone of sea goddesses such as Amphitrite, wife of the Greek sea-god Poseidon, and Aphrodite, the Greek Venus, who was born from the foam of the sea. In the past, sailors carried the stone as a talisman to protect them when they were away from home, and to save them from drowning. With its special connection to water, cleansing the stone in the ocean in the full moon can be a very powerful process.

Aquamarine's vibration resonates with water energy, so this is a lovely stone to use in the bathroom to create an oasis of calm and harmonize the existing energies there.

Crystal energizing

As the bathroom needs to be a sanctuary, a retreat where you can cleanse and soak away the worries of the day, it is good to place a peaceful crystal here that can also purify the atmosphere and keep it balanced. Take your aquamarine in your hands and ask it to let its peaceful and uplifting emanations fill the room at all times and remove any pollutants there. Place the stone on the side of the bath so that you can admire it and enjoy its comforting qualities and let it release your stress and worries while bathing. If you have had a tough day, you can rub the stone over your body to cleanse you of all irritations.

ALTERNATIVE HARMONIZING CRYSTALS TO USE

Turquoise: an empathetic stone that removes any pollutants and equalizes room's energies

Blue lace agate: its cooling and calming vibrations bring relaxation

Bathing with rose quartz to heal and soothe emotions

Rose quartz cleanses the emotions, promotes inner healing, and allows self-love to flow freely. When used in crystal divination, rose quartz can signal a time of healing, or indicate the presence of our ability to heal ourselves and other people.

Rough

A rose quartz can help whenever you are dealing with emotional problems that leave your mind disturbed and your feelings fragile. A major argument at work, coping with a demanding elderly relative, or falling out with a friend can all make you feel vulnerable, upset, and demoralized. It is essential to take some time out to review your feelings. Using a healing crystal in your bath can help you regain your self-worth and support the healing process.

CRYSTAL FACTS

CRYSTAL TO USE: rose quartz (pink), translucent, sometimes tumbled

AVAILABILITY: commonly available

QUALITIES OF STONE: takes away negative energy and replaces with loving vibrations, reduces tensions, aids forgiveness

WHERE TO PLACE THE CRYSTAL: in the bath

Crystal cure

After a traumatic day, a long soak in the bath with a nurturing crystal can be just what you need the most. First set the scene: light an aromatherapy oil burner and add a few drops of lavender or geranium essential oil to the water bowl to relax you (remember, don't leave the burner unattended). Run a warm bath, then place the stone in the water for a few minutes before getting in. Step into the bath and sense the loving energies that are surrounding you. Take your stone and hold it to your heart for a few minutes. Place it back in the bath and rest there for another 5 minutes. Step out of the bath emotionally renewed, remove your crystal, and thank it for its loving work. If you have used an oil burner, extinguish the flame.

ALTERNATIVE SOOTHING CRYSTALS TO USE

Rhodochrosite: heals emotional wounds, encourages acceptance

Tiger's eye: grounds and balances emotions, enhances insight (right: red tiger's eye)

Moonstone: lessens overreaction, soothes emotions (right: polished opaque moonstone)

Focusing concentration with lapis lazuli

Rough

Lapis lazuli is a spiritual crystal that opens up your intuition and psychic abilities. People call it the "eye of wisdom" or the "stone of the gods," as it activates the Third eye chakra: the place of inner learning. The healing power of lapis is well documented in references to jewelry over 3,000 years ago in ancient Egyptian papyri. The ancient Egyptians also appreciated the protective power of the stone, crushing it to make a vivid blue eye powder to guard against the evil eye.

As a beautiful deep blue, opaque stone, lapis lazuli often has inclusions of pretty gold pyrite that catch the light. Mental clarity and objectivity come to you when you handle it, giving the necessary focus and concentration needed when studying for an examination, or assimilating complex information for a diploma course.

CRYSTAL FACTS

CRYSTAL TO USE: lapis lazuli (blue with gold flecks; may be blue and white [white is calcite]; may have black spots of lazulite)

AVAILABILITY: commonly available

QUALITIES OF STONE: brings objectivity and mental clarity, boosts self-confidence, stimulates the mind's faculties, helps to express opinions, amplifies your thoughts

WHERE TO PLACE THE CRYSTAL: place on desk in front of you

Polished

Crystal energizing

Taking an examination can mean expressing acquired knowledge. Using your lapis stone can focus your attention and give you easier access to your inner wisdom. To get the crystal to work with you, take it in your hands and connect to its psychic emanations, asking for its help to stimulate your learning and to amplify your thoughts. Feel the crystal firing up your mental concentration. Now let the stone nurture you as you start to assimilate more text. For essay writing, feel it helping you to find the words to write persuasively.

ALTERNATIVE STUDYING CRYSTALS TO USE

Calcite: stimulates memory, helps to retain important information

Fluorite: helps absorb new information, aids concentration (right: green fluorite)

Creating new ideas with purple fluorite

Fluorite is an attractive transparent crystal that is coming into its own once again, and is considered one of the "New Age" stones. One variety of this colorful crystal resembles two pyramids fused together. In magic spells, fluorite is an amplifier, strengthening the effects of all the crystals used. A powerful cleanser of the environment, purple fluorite also works on the mind, stimulating mental powers, regulating thought patterns, and revealing new ideas. It is an ideal crystal to spark off a productive brain-storming session at home, pitching new topics as a lecturer or self-employed writer.

Rough

Crystal energizing

Purple fluorite helps get you out of a mental rut. So when creativity is diminishing, pick up your crystal and hold it in your hands to tune into its mental powers. Sense how the stone is clearing and energizing your mind. Now say an appropriate affirmation 20 times, such as: "My mind is full of original feature ideas," or, "I am brimming with many interesting subjects for my lectures." Let your stone work with you mentally, fixing this affirmation in your subconscious. Now turn on your computer and put your crystal beside it. Feel its vibrations increasing your vision, and start typing out the new angles or approaches that are beginning to flow through you.

CRYSTAL FACTS

CRYSTAL TO USE: purple fluorite, transparent, cubic or octahedral

AVAILABILITY: commonly available

QUALITIES OF STONE: helps you come up with abstract ideas, focuses energy, expands mental capabilities, enhances creativity, promotes fast thinking

WHERE TO PLACE THE CRYSTAL: in your hands and by computer

Polished

ALTERNATIVE CREATIVITY CRYSTALS TO USE

Aventurine: offers alternatives, increases perception and creativity

Bloodstone: enhances creative decision-making, strengthens intuition

Citrine: revitalizes the mind, stimulates creativity

Aiding difficult self-expression with blue celestite

Rough

CRYSTAL FACTS

Crystal to use: blue celestite, transparent, medium to large cluster, or geode

Availability: commonly available

Qualities of stone: expands the consciousness, opens Throat chakra, heightens telepathic abilities, soothes nerves, creates honesty, sharpens the mind, promotes good communication, cools fiery emotions

Where to place the crystal: on Throat chakra in the middle of your throat and in your pocket

Celestite is a stunning, light blue crystal that is associated with the goddess Venus. The crystal clusters can be quite brittle, so it is not often used to make jewelry. A versatile gem, when ground it is used to make caustic soda, and the salts of red celestite are used to add the color red to fireworks and flares, and in the preparation of iridescent glass and porcelain. Blue celestite is, however, a soothing stone, bringing harmony to a troubled mind and easing stress. Its gentle blue rays open the Throat energetic chakra, easing any of your current communication problems. Running a home office can involve resolving problems with plumbers or electricians or may involve querying your bills. When this happens, use your celestite crystal to express what you truly want to say.

Crystal energizing

Blue celestite deals with speaking the truth, helping you to speak your mind in a subtle but positive way. To resolve a communication problem, hold the crystal and feel its cooling energy. Place it on your throat chakra for 5–10 minutes or so, feeling how these pure vibrations are dissolving any blockages and harmonizing the energy here. You may find yourself coughing a bit as the energy shifts. Now keep the crystal in your pocket as you prepare to deal with the tradesperson who has been causing a problem. Let the crystal's calming vibrations help you to make your point assertively.

ALTERNATIVE DIFFICULT SELF-EXPRESSION CRYSTALS TO USE

Blue lace agate: helps expression of thoughts without anger

Blue kyanite: lessens fear and encourages speaking difficult truths

Sodalite: helps with rational thought and saying true feelings

Crystal first-aid for phone stress

If you work from home, your main form of communication with the outside world, aside from email, is by phone. As pressure builds on busy projects, some calls can become tense as you are asked to do several things at once. Keeping a special mix of carefully chosen de-stressing crystals by the phone can give you some protection from the debilitating vibrations of negative people or emotional vampires, helping you handle difficult situations without losing your temper.

Crystal cure

Placing these colorful healing crystals by the phone can act as an emotional first-aid kit. The grounding qualities of these stones can give you emotional support when you are doing too much, and create a harmonious atmosphere that will influence your work area. Buy the crystals as smooth tumbled stones so that when you feel yourself getting upset or angry during a difficult phone call, you can turn over the relevant crystal in your hand. The green healing qualities of aventurine will take away your anger, leaving a feeling of wellbeing. When a tricky client is frustrating you, pick up a stone such as amethyst and feel its high spiritual vibration protecting you from their emotional debris, or use bloodstone to repel their negative vibes or undesirable comments. Always cleanse your crystals every few weeks (see pages 149–153), particularly if you have experienced several fraught conversations.

CRYSTAL FACTS

CRYSTALS TO USE: choose two crystals from each of the groups below:

> **Calming:** agate, aquamarine, howlite, selenite
>
> **Stress-relieving:** amber, blue kyanite, smoky quartz
>
> **Anger-defusing:** blue lace agate, green aventurine, peridot, red garnet
>
> **Protective:** amethyst, bloodstone, brown jasper, carnelian

AVAILABILITY: commonly available

QUALITIES OF STONES: using a selection of these crystals brings emotional balance, calms the mind, alleviates stress, reduces frustration, neutralizes anger and irritation, protects against psychic attack, forms a protective barrier, grounds energies

WHERE TO PLACE THE CRYSTALS: in a bowl by the phone

Fostering a nurturing atmosphere with rhodonite

Polished

This pretty pink stone, mottled with black, can enhance the nurturing vibrations in the kitchen, the heart of the home. Family disputes will not last long in a kitchen that contains a rhodonite crystal, because rhodonite grounds energy, balancing yin and yang—the opposing passive and positive forces in the universe. This in turn helps balance any emotional outbursts, and thankfully encourages a spirit of forgiveness. Rhodonite and other pink crystals, such as rose quartz and rhodochrosite (see pages 78 and 104), are also associated with generating physical love and affection, and this stone radiates a warm, caring vibration that instil a nonconfrontational ambience wherever it is placed.

CRYSTAL FACTS

CRYSTAL TO USE: rhodonite (red or pink), mottled effect, sometimes flecked with black and/or white

AVAILABILITY: commonly available

QUALITIES OF STONE: reduces stress, increases energy levels, stimulates a peaceful and loving atmosphere, balances emotions, encourages good interaction between people

WHERE TO PLACE THE CRYSTAL: on kitchen table or shelf

Crystal energizing
Pick up your crystal and connect with its emissions of unconditional love. Ask it to make your kitchen a comfort zone, a place of conviviality and laughter where meals are lovingly prepared and eaten. Now place the crystal in a glass bowl in the center of the kitchen table, or put it on a prominent shelf above the countertops to let it do its tender work.

ALTERNATIVE NURTURING CRYSTALS TO USE

Jade: protects the room, creates a serene, harmonious atmosphere (right: polished egg)

Green tourmaline: energizes, bringing a balanced and joyful ambience

Rose quartz: creates an empathetic and loving energy

Preventing accidents with moss agate

Known as the most powerful of the agates, moss agate was the chosen talisman worn by warriors going into battle. It is a highly protective crystal that can stabilize the fiery energy associated with stovetops and kitchen cookers, giving out a lovely healing aura. The wonderful color of the stone is also associated with maternal love, reminding us that special care needs to be taken in the kitchen, where most accidents in the home happen. The deep green color of moss agate also reduces any stress when cooking meals and creates a strong feeling of security.

Polished

CRYSTAL FACTS

CRYSTAL TO USE: green moss agate, transparent or translucent, has foliage-like markings

AVAILABILITY: commonly available

QUALITIES OF STONE: very protective, encourages a long life, reduces sensitivity to any environmental pollutants, soothes emotions

WHERE TO PLACE THE CRYSTAL: place near stovetop or cooker, or other accident hot spot

Crystal cure

Take hold of this attractive crystal in your hands and connect to its grounding earth energies. Ask the stone to protect your kitchen, keeping negative influences out, and preventing accidents such as cuts and burns. Place the stone close to your cooktop and food preparation area, so that its healing green rays span out around the space where you do your food preparation and cooking. Cleanse the crystal regularly (see pages 149–153) to keep its energies vital.

ALTERNATIVE PROTECTIVE CRYSTALS TO USE

Bloodstone: grounding and protective stone, revitalizes atmosphere

Lavender (purple) jade: protects from harm, brings harmony

Malachite: protects and absorbs negative energies and pollutants

Keeping vegetables and fruit fresh with aqua aura quartz

This beautiful crystal is artificially made; a secret alchemical process bonds a quartz crystal with pure gold, resulting in the striking color of aqua aura. The color is similar to aquamarine, and has an opalescence that flashes wonderful shades of blue (or purple, if the crystal has been overheated during the process). The combination of a crystal and a precious mineral makes a high and intense energetic vibration that is ideal to increase the life force and preserve the vitamin and mineral content of fresh fruits and vegetables. The high electric charge of quartz has been proven through Kirlian photography, where an infrared image of the crystal is taken, showing its energetic field.

Crystal energizing

Use aqua aura crystals with a terminated point or a cluster with obvious points so that you can direct the energy toward the food you want to preserve. Pick up your crystals one by one and hold them in your hands briefly, asking them to keep your food fresher for longer. Now place the crystals permanently at each corner of your fruit bowl, with the points facing inward or around your vegetable basket and see how bright and vibrant the food stays. If you are preparing a meal, point one crystal toward the ingredients as you chop them up to boost their freshness.

CRYSTAL FACTS

Crystal to use: Four blue aqua aura quartz, terminated points, or a cluster. Aqua aura is artificially bonded with gold to create varying strong color

Availability: commonly available

Qualities of stone: powers of gold and quartz greatly amplify energy, help to preserve and heal, work at the vibrational level needed, preserve food and plants

Where to place the crystal: around vegetables and fruit

Purple aqua aura

Enjoying convivial dining with a crystal centerpiece

Although technically not a true crystal, lead-faceted glass crystal has been known as a powerful energizer. As the light refracts through the cut glass, it brings a charge of energy. The round shape, or circle, of the bowl is universally revered. It symbolically represents eternity, unity, and the universe, the goddess and female power, and Mother Earth. In Chinese traditions a round bowl signifies abundance, so by placing this vibrant centerpiece on your dining table you are making a statement of abundance, saying that there is plenty of food and fun in store for your guests.

CRYSTAL FACTS

CRYSTAL TO USE: wide and shallow lead-faceted crystal bowl

QUALITIES OF BOWL: amplifies and regulates energy in a similar way to natural quartz

WHERE TO PLACE THE BOWL: in the center of the dining table

Crystal energizing

To make your table centerpiece really stand out, buy a shallow, wide bowl with an attractive pattern, so that the facets will catch the light from every angle, making the room feel vibrant and vital.

On the night of the dinner party, fill the bowl with water, add a sprinkling of pretty flower petals, and place some white floating candles on top. The strong fire energy from the candles will also encourage a lively atmosphere. Light the candles just before the guests sit down for dinner to create the maximum effect.

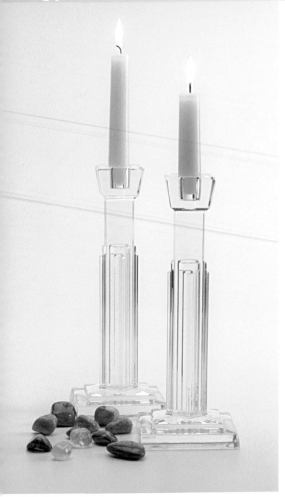

Romantic dining with lead-crystal candlesticks and red stones

If you are in a new, ardent relationship or have been together for some time, a romantic dinner can reinforce your feelings for each other. Placing lead-faceted glass candlesticks on the table creates a *frisson* as the facets of the glass catch the light, lifting and expanding the chi, or energy, in the atmosphere. Scattering stimulating red and pink crystals around the candles helps to open up your Heart chakras, or centers of love, bringing in empathetic and passionate vibrations that will make it a meal where you only have eyes for each other.

Crystal energizing

Place the lead-crystal candlesticks in the center of the table. Use pink candles, because pink inspires unconditional love, or white candles, which represent purity. Choose red and pink crystals to symbolize your love, energizing them before dinner for 24 hours in the moonlight (see page 154), calling on the beautiful Roman moon goddess Diana to bless your love and make it last. You can use heart-shaped stones, if you can find them.

Just before dinner, pick up each chosen crystal individually: they all link to the stimulating Fire element. Feel each one's caring and affectionate pulsations: red garnet will stir up passion and feelings of devotion, while pink rhodochrosite strengthens a burgeoning relationship and boosts sexuality. Ask each stone to use its special powers to surround you with a loving and tender embrace for the whole evening.

CRYSTAL FACTS

Crystals to use: lead-faceted crystal candlesticks and choose three from the following red and pink crystals:

Red for passion: opal with red inclusions (pure red opal is rare in most countries), red garnet, ruby

Pink for love: rose quartz, pink agate, rhodochrosite, rhodonite

Availability: commonly available

Qualities: the candlesticks lift the vibrancy of the room. Red and pink crystals inspire love and devotion, romantic inclinations, increase passion and sexual potency, and inspire the emotions

Where to place: in the center of the table

Deflecting negativity from colleagues with smoky quartz

Smoky quartz is a protective crystal with a brownish hue. Its dark color is normally caused by radiation and the presence of carbon, iron, or titanium impurities. The stone is said to lose its dark color and become almost clear as you work through the negativity and problems in your life. Its unique vibration helps you cope with difficult times, and it has the ability to block any unwanted vibrations around you—so it's a potent stone to use at work when you need to deflect any backbiting or unpleasant gossiping from colleagues.

Smoky quartz wand

Crystal cure

As many office environments today are open-plan, it is inevitable that you will be influenced by the energies of the people sitting close to you. To deflect any negativity, take hold of your smoky quartz crystal for a few minutes, feeling its reasssuring aura. Ask it to form a protective barrier around you so that your energy field is not depleted by any malicious talk or action. Place the crystal on your desk and turn its protective point toward the people with the most negative attitudes. Always cleanse the crystal regularly (see pages 149–153) so that it works at its highest level.

CRYSTAL FACTS

CRYSTAL TO USE: a long, pointed smoky quartz crystal (brown/black), transparent

QUALITIES OF STONE: protects and dissolves negativity on all levels, grounds and centers, aids meditation, cleanses and protects the aura (energetic field), lifts moods, relieves stress, blocks geopathic and electromagnetic stress, alleviates fear and depression

HEALTH BENEFITS: aids functioning of the kidneys, adrenal glands, and pancreas, balances sexual energy, increases fertility, relieves problems in abdomen, hips, and legs, good pain reliever, eases headaches, reduces cramps, strengthens the back

WHERE TO PLACE THE CRYSTAL: on your desk

ALTERNATIVE ANTI-NEGATIVITY CRYSTALS TO USE

Fire agate: grounds and protects, forms a shield around body

Amber: protects, absorbs any negative forces, and cleanses environment

Labradorite: deflects unwanted negativity, gets rid of fear and insecurities (right: polished egg)

Dispelling computer stress with fluorite

Polished
yellow/green
banded

Polished green/blue
purple banded

Polished
purple

CRYSTAL FACTS

CRYSTAL TO USE: fluorite (clear, blue, green, purple, yellow, brown), transparent

AVAILABILITY: commonly available

QUALITIES OF STONE: removes negative energies, dispels electromagnetic stress from computers

WHERE TO PLACE THE CRYSTAL: by or on your computer

Although little is known of its ritual use, fluorite, which was found in the ruins of Pompeii, has been with us since ancient times. Today, crystal healers use it as a stone of purification and protection. You can use fluorite at home or the office to absorb electromagnetic radiation from computers, and also to lift the overall energy levels in your work space.

Computer screens emit electromagnetic radiation, most of which is filtered by the screens, but this efficiency decreases as computers age. This radiation can make you feel lethargic, tired, and debilitated. The screen also gives out positive ions that can make your eyes very dry and sore. If you're suffering from any of these symptoms, fluorite may help; this stone is strongly protective, and it will remove any existing negative energies.

Crystal cure

Hold the crystal in your hand briefly and ask it to improve the atmosphere of your working environment before placing it on top of your computer or close by it. The fluorite will be hard at work every time you use your computer, so cleanse the stone regularly (see pages 149–153). You can also place a plant such as a peace lily or peperomia next to your computer to filter the air, increase negative ionization, and protect you from daily radiation emissions.

ALTERNATIVE COMPUTER STRESS-RELIEVING CRYSTALS TO USE

Smoky quartz: detoxifies and soaks up electromagnetic radiation

Black tourmaline: protects against negative energies and electromagnetic emissions

Amazonite: powerful filtering stone, removes electromagnetic pollution

Encouraging career achievement with natural quartz cluster

Natural quartz is a wonderful amplifier, stimulating brain activity, helping to formulate action and support your career needs. A quartz cluster, comprising many mini points and facets, has the ability to transmit positive energy while absorbing negative vibes—so if you have a tendency to doubt your abilities, this sparkling crystal formation can remove your indecision and instill you with confidence.

If you are finding it difficult to be recognized for your achievements, you can add a little feng shui to help you gain the success you desire.

Cluster

CRYSTAL FACTS

CRYSTAL TO USE: natural quartz cluster (clear or milky)

AVAILABILITY: commonly available

QUALITIES OF STONE: powerful energizer, tunes in to the person using the stone, boosts concentration

WHERE TO PLACE THE CRYSTAL: in the northeast section of your desk

Crystal energizing

The northeast of your desk is the best place to position your natural quartz cluster. It is your Education and knowledge area, so the crystal will support the earth energies existing in this space. Spend some time attuning to your

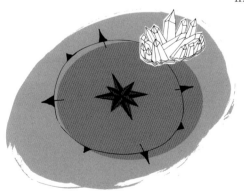

crystal's vibrations before you place it. Program it for what you desire next in your career. Be very specific in your aims and the stone will work with you to lift the energetic frequency around you so that you gain what you want.

If you can, place your telephone in the south area of your desk—this is your Fame area, which again can enhance your chances of doing well.

Bringing success in meetings with green agate

Rough

An agate is a wonderful crystal for increasing mental powers and improving your perceptive skills. Its talent for aiding analysis was well known in Asia in the past, where a scryer would gaze into the stone to try to discover future trends.

If business meetings are a regular part of your working life, and making a positive impact or handling a presentation successfully is important to your career, an agate can give you the confidence to handle yourself well. Using it can increase your resolve and business acumen, keeping you "on your toes" so that you have ready answers to any tricky questions.

CRYSTAL FACTS

CRYSTAL TO USE: green agate. Can be sold artificially colored, which is often banded

AVAILABILITY: commonly available

QUALITIES OF STONE: boosts ego and self-esteem, increases energy, strengthens mind, improves concentration and brain function, gives mental flexibility

WHERE TO PLACE THE CRYSTAL: in your pocket, or hold in your hand

Polished

Crystal energizing

Before your meeting starts, sit at your desk and pick up your green agate. Hold it tightly for about 5 minutes, tuning in to its vibrations as the stone gives you courage and self-respect. Feel the soothing green color calming your nerves and stabilizing your heart rate. Ask the stone for its help to make you speak eloquently at your meeting. Let it work on increasing your self-worth so that your meeting is a success. Put your green agate in your pocket, and enter your meeting positively with a relaxed smile.

ALTERNATIVE SUCCESS CRYSTALS TO USE

Tiger's eye: recognizes inner resources, promotes clarity of intention

Carnelian: encourages vitality, motivation and business success

Chrysoprase: stimulates fluent speech and versatile reasoning

Keeping away computer viruses with malachite

Malachite is a transformational crystal that lets you live life more intensely under its influence. Some people believe it will become one of the most prized healing stones of this century. Malachite is reputed to help with spiritual development and inner journeying; it is also very protective—those who use it regularly say that it breaks into pieces when danger is near.

Placed on your desk, malachite will soak up some of the electromagnetic pollution emitted by your computer and other appliances. You can make it your own personal guardian against viruses that can attack your computer via the internet and email. Its healing energy can be an added repellent to any new viruses that are attacking software programs and can be used alongside your dedicated anti-virus program. The stone dispels negativity, absorbing any radiation and pollutants that leak into the atmosphere.

Crystal cure

Pick up your stone and hold it firmly in your hand to feel its power and purifying abilities. Ask it to soak up any negativity from your office space and send out strong, positive energetic rays around your computer to keep it virus-free. Circle the stone around the computer twice daily, morning and late afternoon. Cleanse the stone after each use under running water, or see pages 149–153.

CRYSTAL FACTS

CRYSTAL TO USE: malachite (green with black); when tumbled, shows light and dark bands; best to use polished malachite as dust from rough crystal can adversely affect some people

AVAILABILITY: commonly available

QUALITIES OF STONE: reduces negativity and eases depression, alleviates stress and tension, protects against negative energies and electromagnetic emissions, aids sleep, promotes business success, brings transformation

WHERE TO PLACE THE CRYSTAL: on your desk

Dealing with confrontation with blue moonstone

A blue moonstone, also known as rainbow moonstone, with its lovely pearly sheen may appear otherworldly—it is believed to be a stone of prophecy under a full moon— yet it is clearly a crystal for this material world. It teaches us that love is important: a message that will get through to even the hardest cynic. A stone of balance, moonstone regulates both male and female energies, letting anyone get in touch with their feminine side and become more empathetic. Linked to the moon's cycles, it helps to soothe your own rollercoaster of emotions and keeps stress levels down. The moonstone is also known for its conciliatory qualities, so keeping it on your desk can create a neutral zone in office politics.

CRYSTAL FACTS

CRYSTAL TO USE: blue moonstone, blue and cloudy-white, translucent, often with black inclusions

AVAILABILITY: commonly available

QUALITIES OF STONE: helps to balance emotions, dissipates anxiety and stress, calms aggression and overreactions in arguments, encourages flexibility in attitudes

WHERE TO PLACE THE CRYSTAL: in your pocket or on your desk, or wear it as jewelry

In fraught situations with colleagues, this sensitive stone builds an empathetic shield around you.

Crystal cure

If an office confrontation does occur, pick up your stone and hold it tightly in your hand, until you feel its passive energy stabilizing and healing your emotions, defusing your anger, and stopping you overreacting to the disagreement. Cleanse regularly to keep it vibrant (see pages 149–153).

ALTERNATIVE NON-CONFRONTATIONAL CRYSTALS TO USE

Celestite: peaceful stone that improves adversarial relationships

Jasper: gives support in conflict, encourages resolve (right: red jasper)

Pietersite: supportive stone that helps solve conflicts

Stopping constant interruptions with amethyst

Amethyst is a very spiritual crystal but has the transformational properties of natural quartz. A highly protective stone that was worn by ancient Egyptian soldiers to calm their fears in battle, amethyst can become your talisman at work. With reports to write, meetings to prepare for, and a multitude of emails to answer, the last thing you want when your time is limited is to be constantly interrupted by colleagues. A pointed amethyst crystal is wonderful to have on your desk as it supports your endeavors, soothes any worries or anxieties every time you gaze at it, while also repelling any unwanted visitors when you are desperate to meet a deadline.

Crystal cure

Hold the crystal in your hands and ask it to create a protective shield around you, then place it on your desk with the point facing the wall. Whenever you see someone approaching that you do not want to speak to, turn the point around to face them, and then watch how they stop, look a bit puzzled, and then go off in another direction. This gentle crystal will not harm them but they will not want to walk through its barrier. Cleanse it regularly to remove negativity (see pages 149–153).

Amethyst wand

CRYSTAL FACTS

CRYSTAL TO USE: amethyst (violet/purple), transparent, single point or wand

AVAILABILITY: commonly available

QUALITIES OF STONE: healing and calming, protects, soothes the mind, rebalances emotions, blocks negative environmental energies, gives focus and mental stability, strengthens memory and increases motivation

WHERE TO PLACE THE CRYSTAL: in your pocket, or on your desk

ALTERNATIVE PROTECTIVE CRYSTALS TO USE

Rose quartz: creates a loving barrier, promotes sensitivity

Natural quartz: makes a strong energetic field, works to your purpose

Black tourmaline: protects and repels negative energies

Connecting with inner wisdom with lapis lazuli

Rough

Lapis lazuli was revered by ancient cultures such as the Sumerians, who believed it contained souls of their gods and goddesses, and that if they wore the stone they would become godlike and able to perform magical powers. A mystical crystal, lapis creates inner and outer harmony of the mind, body, and spirit.

When your life seems to be a series of setbacks, lapis helps you take charge of your life. Mentally, it stops you from feeling so stressed and gives you coping strategies when you run into difficulties at work, particularly when you feel that you have run out of solutions and ideas. Lapis lazuli's special protective wisdom shifts your mental blocks and lets you tap into your intuition to gain the guidance you need.

CRYSTAL FACTS

CRYSTAL TO USE: lapis lazuli (blue with gold flecks; may be blue and white [white is calcite]; may have black spots of lazulite)

AVAILABILITY: commonly available, but can be expensive

QUALITIES OF STONE: helps psychic development and intuition, brings mental stability and clarity, alleviates stress, balances physical, mental and emotional feelings, helps objectivity and clarity

WHERE TO PLACE THE CRYSTAL: on your Third eye chakra in the middle of your forehead

Crystal energizing

To source your answers, sit in a quiet space, close your eyes, and place your lapis lazuli crystal on your Third eye chakra: just touching the stone is believed to improve your mental and emotional situation. Breathe deeply and semi-meditate as you concentrate on your problem, saying mentally, "I am finding the solution I need right now." Feel this creative crystal's vibrations allowing you to access your subconscious and inner wisdom. Sit for several minutes until you sense the answers you want flowing in.

ALTERNATIVE INTUITIVE CRYSTALS TO USE

Amber: encourages wisdom and inspired self-expression

Topaz: helps tap into your inner psyche for knowledge

Onyx: helps you go inside and make wise decisions

Achieving goals with golden topaz

The word topaz may have derived from the ancient Sanskrit word *tapas*, meaning "fire." This lovely yellow crystal is an instant energizer, giving you the charisma to find the success and fame you seek. Its generosity is supposed to bring wealth and money into your life. This power of attraction can also help you attain the goals you set yourself at work. Goals are important in your working life to move you on in your career and prevent lethargy from setting in. Choosing a goal will give you focus. Everyone's goals are different: you may want promotion in a year. Other people may want to take a year out and work abroad, or need to pass an important examination. Golden topaz can connect you to your inner wisdom and help you reach your goal.

Crystal energizing

Choose your goal. If you are having problems deciding, think of each option in turn and sense which one gives you a warm sensation and feels right, even if it is a bit frightening. Use your golden topaz crystal at the full moon or when it is waxing to receive its full powers. Now pick up your stone and hold it in your hands or over your solar plexus for about 5 minutes, releasing any blockages or upsets held there, and ask for its assistance in achieving your aim. Concentrate hard on your goal, feeling the vibrations coming out of your stone as it works on boosting you physically to give you the presence you need to follow your dream.

Polished

CRYSTAL FACTS

CRYSTAL TO USE: golden topaz, transparent, tumbled, or sometimes pointed and faceted

AVAILABILITY: commonly available from specialist stores

QUALITIES OF STONE: recharges and motivates, develops intuition, strengthens nervous system, promotes self-realization and inner awareness, helps to communicate ideas and recognize own abilities

WHERE TO PLACE THE CRYSTAL: in your hands or over your heart

ALTERNATIVE GOAL-ACHIEVING CRYSTALS TO USE

Dendritic agate: brings abundance in business, aids perseverance (right: moss agate)

Carnelian: good for business success, increases motivation

Fire opal: stimulates personal power, brings progress

Reducing work frustration with blue kyanite

Rough

The word kyanite comes from the Greek word *kyanos,* meaning "blue," which is the principal color of this crystal. This flat-bladed crystal with a pearly covering is often unevenly colored, with the strongest blue tints in the middle. Its high spiritual frequencies can stimulate your psychic awareness and increase your intuition and problem-solving abilities. Psychologically, it calms and takes away trifling worries, reminding you that everything happens for a reason. Kyanite does not hold negativity, so is invaluable to keep as a soothing desk accessory to dispel the anger of a confrontation with your boss, or other stresses or difficult tasks that can build up during a normal working day.

Crystal cure

Working flat out for weeks on end can leave you mentally drained, with a tendency to overreact to any unforeseen problems that occur. Performing a short daily meditation for about 10 minutes at lunchtime with kyanite can release these frustrations, giving you increased mental clarity and perception. Sit in a quiet space holding your crystal in your hands. Breathe in deeply and as you breathe out let out all your stress and tension. Gaze into your crystal, noticing its beauty, shape, and color. As your mind slows with your breathing, feel the crystal's amplifying vibrations deepening your meditation, bringing light to your soul, and slowing you down so that you can see the right solutions to your problems. Slowly come back to the room.

CRYSTAL FACTS

CRYSTAL TO USE: blue kyanite transparent or opaque, sometimes striated

AVAILABILITY: commonly available

QUALITIES OF STONE: aids meditation, inspires loyalty, clears mind, allows new thought patterns, increases creative self-expression, increases psychic abilities and intuition, dispels energy blockages, dispels anger, frustration, and worry

HEALTH BENEFITS: works on thyroid, parathyroid and adrenal glands, lowers blood pressure, helps to heal infections

WHERE TO PLACE THE CRYSTAL: hold in hands

ALTERNATIVE WORRY-RELEASING CRYSTALS TO USE

Amazonite: calms the brain, lets you see both sides of a problem

Onyx: relieves fears and worries, encourages wise decisions

Apophyllite: releases stress, aids decision-making process

Creating inner harmony with a natural quartz pendulum

Faceted quartz pendulum

Problem

If you are out of sorts, lethargic or lacking enthusiasm, one or several chakras can be out of balance.

Solution

Dowsing with a natural quartz pendulum, a powerful energy amplifier, can find the energetic imbalance. You can then correct the chakra or chakras by using the right color of crystal for that area.

Cleansing your energy

If you are feeling run-down, here's how to test the health of your chakras:

1. Half-lie on a mat on the floor, holding your natural quartz pendulum in your dominant hand. Check the Root chakra by holding the quartz pendulum over your lower pelvis. When healthy, the crystal reacts to the normal vibration by spinning counterclockwise for a woman (clockwise for a man); if it swings from side to side the crystal has detected an energetic problem.

2. Now work up the chakras. They function like cogs in a wheel, so the second chakra, the Sacral, should spin clockwise (counterclockwise for a man) and the next one clockwise, and so on.

3. Check all the chakras, noting down any unhealthy ones, then treat them with the appropriate color of crystal (see pages 58–64).

Chakra positions

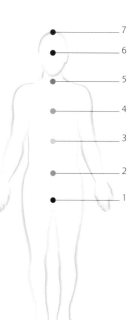

The body has seven principal chakras, or energy centers, which are situated in your etheric body, the energy-layer that surrounds the physical body.

1 Root, lower pelvic area
2 Sacral, pelvic area
3 Solar plexus, upper abdomen
4 Heart, middle of chest
5 Throat, middle of throat
6 Third eye, middle of forehead
7 Crown, top of head

CRYSTAL FACTS

CRYSTAL TO USE: natural quartz pendulum with chain

AVAILABILITY: commonly available from crystal stores

QUALITIES OF STONE: powerful healer, amplifies and transmits energy, aligns the energy requirements of person needing healing, dissolves negativity in energy field, increases intuition

WORKING ON: all the chakras

HEALTH BENEFITS: heals any ailment, brings body back in balance, relieves burns, soothes toothache

HOW A PENDULUM WORKS: dowsing with a pendulum is an ancient technique that can check the vibrational frequency of the chakras. A malfunction is detected by a change in the pendulum's movement

How to be more grounded with bloodstone

Polished

CRYSTAL FACTS

CRYSTAL TO USE: bloodstone, also known as heliotrope, is a type of green jasper that contains red spots of iron oxide. Although mainly green, this grounding stone resonates with the Root chakra

AVAILABILITY: commonly available

QUALITIES OF STONE: links Root chakra with heart, gives vitality, strengthens idealistic views, alleviates emotional stress, increases courage to revive an exhausted mind, a grounding and protective stone

WORKING ON: Root chakra at the base of the spine (or around pubic area on front of body)

COLOR NEEDED BY CHAKRA: red

PARTS OF BODY AFFECTED BY CRYSTAL: adrenal glands, lower pelvic area

HEALTH BENEFITS: strengthens blood circulation, corrects iron deficiencies, detoxifies liver, kidneys, intestines, and spleen, increases metabolism

WHERE TO PLACE THE CRYSTAL: hold over the lower pelvis

Problem

If you are not feeling rooted in your existence, or if your instincts are down, the energy in your lower pelvis will not be up to full strength.

Solution

To feel more grounded, or down to earth, you will need to work on the Root chakra: the first energy center (see page 57).

Boost your energy

The Root chakra is also the area of self-preservation, associated with our instincts to keep away from danger. To stimulate the flow of energy to this center or remove a blockage, lie on your back in a calm room. Pick up your bloodstone crystal and tune in to its power to cleanse you energetically. Close your eyes and place or hold the crystal on your Root chakra for 5 minutes by holding or resting it on your lower pelvis. Contemplate your grounding problem, allowing your stimulating red crystal to harmonize and revitalize the energies existing here, then slowly come back into the room. Cleanse the stone (see pages 149–153). Work with this crystal daily for one or two weeks until life no longer feels a burden and you feel more fixed in your own skin.

The Root chakra and symbol

ALTERNATIVE GROUNDING CRYSTALS TO USE

Smoky quartz: solid and grounding; increases resolve, relieves fear (right: with rutiles)

Agate: grounding, healing stone that brings balance (right: brown agate)

Onyx: imparts self-control and encourages a less "airy" existence

Boosting your creativity with orange calcite

Problem

If you feel that you have lost the ability to be creative, or your life lacks fulfillment, the energy in the middle part of your body will be depleted.

Solution

To increase your creativity levels, you will benefit from doing some crystal work on your Sacral chakra: the second spiritual energy center (see page 57).

Rough

Boost your energy

The Sacral chakra is also the area that controls your sexuality, security, and how you see the world. To increase or balance the energy flow to this area, or to shift a blockage, lie or sit down comfortably in a quiet room, pick up your orange calcite crystal and sense your connection with this energizing stone. Close your eyes and place or hold the crystal on your Sacral chakra for 5 minutes, then focus on your creativity problem and let the crystal do its work, correcting your energetic level. Work with this warming crystal energy daily for one or two weeks until you start to feel a surge of new creativity and optimism bubbling up inside you.

The Sacral, or navel, chakra and symbol

CRYSTAL FACTS

CRYSTAL TO USE: orange calcite, translucent, may be banded

AVAILABILITY: commonly available

QUALITIES OF STONE: stimulates energy, can alleviate fear and stress, strengthens emotions and can build confidence

WORKING ON: Sacral chakra in the pelvic area

COLOR NEEDED BY CHAKRA: orange

PARTS OF BODY AFFECTED BY CRYSTAL: sexual organs, kidneys, bladder, and intestines

HEALTH BENEFITS: cleanses the blood, affects the kidneys, pancreas, and spleen; associated with relieving the symptoms of constipation and diarrhea

WHERE TO PLACE THE CRYSTAL: hold over your pelvic area (just below the navel)

ALTERNATIVE CREATIVITY CRYSTALS TO USE

Amber: promotes joy, takes away negativity

Moonstone: balances emotions, helps new beginnings

Carnelian: alleviates apathy and increases confidence

Increasing your personal power with citrine

Cluster

CRYSTAL FACTS

CRYSTAL TO USE: citrine (yellow, yellow/brown), often a geode point or cluster

AVAILABILITY: natural citrine can be rare; citrine produced by heat-treating amethyst is commonly available

QUALITIES OF STONE: brings happiness and generosity. Increases motivation

WORKING ON: Solar plexus chakra in the upper abdomen

COLOR NEEDED BY CHAKRA: yellow

PARTS OF BODY AFFECTED BY CRYSTAL: pancreas, stomach, spleen, liver

HEALTH BENEFITS: treats digestive problems, thyroid imbalance; increases blood circulation

WHERE TO PLACE THE CRYSTAL: hold over upper abdomen

Problem

When your ego is at a low ebb, if you are suffering an identity crisis, or perhaps you feel your personal power is lacking, the energy in the area just under your chest will be reduced.

Solution

To bring your ego up to full strength, the area to treat with a crystal is your Solar plexus chakra: the third spiritual energy center (see page 57).

Boost your energy

The solar plexus is your area of personal achievement and it relates to speaking out boldly about things that are important to you. To realign the energy flow here, or dissolve a blockage, lie or sit comfortably where you will not be disturbed. Pick up your citrine, and feel your connection to this sunny, joyful stone, then place or hold it on your Solar plexus chakra for 5 minutes. Close your eyes; concentrate on your ego problem as your yellow crystal's stimulating vibrations work on correcting the impulses in this chakra, then slowly come back into the room. Cleanse the stone (see pages 149–153). Use this crystal daily for one or two weeks and notice how your ego is strengthened and how good you now feel about yourself.

The Solar plexus chakra and symbol

ALTERNATIVE PERSONAL POWER CRYSTALS TO USE

Golden topaz: recharges trust and optimism

Golden beryl (heliodor): promotes independent spirit and will to succeed

Rhodochrosite: encourages positive feelings of self-worth

Opening up to love with rose quartz

Rough

Problem

If you have emotionally shut down or you are finding it hard to maintain an intimate, loving relationship, the energy in the middle of your chest will be low.

Solution

To give and receive love once more, you need some crystal energy on your Heart chakra: the fourth energy center (see page 57).

Boost your energy

The Heart chakra is also the place of giving compassion and seeking empathy with other people. To augment, smooth out, or remove a blockage in the energy flow to this center, lie or sit comfortably in a still room and hold your beautiful rose quartz crystal in your hands and feel its gentle, loving pulsations. Close your eyes and place or hold your crystal on your Heart chakra for 5 minutes. Contemplate the lack of love in your life and sense how your purifying and reassuring pink crystal is adjusting the energetic levels here, then slowly come back into the room. Cleanse the stone (see pages 149–153). Use this soothing crystal daily for one or two weeks and see how you much more loving you feel and how much more affectionate you now are with your partner, friends, or family.

The Heart chakra and symbol

CRYSTAL FACTS

CRYSTAL TO USE: rose quartz (pink) translucent or transparent, can be tumbled

AVAILABILITY: commonly available

QUALITIES OF STONE: heals emotional trauma, stimulates friendship, brings peace and unconditional love, promotes compassion and forgiveness, restores trust and harmony, increases self-worth

WORKING ON: Heart chakra in the middle of the chest

COLOR NEEDED BY CHAKRA: green or pink

PARTS OF BODY AFFECTED BY CRYSTAL: thymus, lower lungs, and heart

HEALTH BENEFITS: benefits kidneys, adrenals, and circulatory system, strengthens physical heart, heals cuts or bruises, soothes burns, helps chest and lung ailments

WHERE TO PLACE THE CRYSTAL: hold to heart

ALTERNATIVE LOVE-INCREASING CRYSTALS TO USE

Celestite: dissolves inner pain and lets love in

Rhodochrosite: brings out repressed feelings, opening up the heart to love (rough)

Kunzite: helps to express emotions and awakens unconditional love

How to become more communicative with aquamarine

Polished

CRYSTAL FACTS

CRYSTAL TO USE: aquamarine (green/blue), clear or opaque, sometimes faceted or can be tumbled

AVAILABILITY: commonly available

QUALITIES OF STONE: stimulates self-knowledge, inspires intellect, helps with creative self-expression, balances emotions, reduces stress, stills the mind, encourages understanding of other people

WORKING ON: Throat chakra, in the middle of the throat

COLOR NEEDED BY CHAKRA: turquoise blue

PARTS OF BODY AFFECTED BY CRYSTAL: thyroid and parathyroid, upper lungs, and throat

HEALTH BENEFITS: associated with alleviating toothache, reducing fluid retention, strengthening kidneys, liver, and spleen, soothing sore throats, aiding thyroid problems, helping the body to detox

WHERE TO PLACE THE CRYSTAL: hold to throat

Problem

If you feel you cannot express your true needs or if you are not able to communicate your opinions, the energy in the middle of your throat may be deficient.

Solution

To open up your communication channels, the area that will gain from some crystal work is your Throat chakra: the fifth energy center (see page 57).

Boost your energy

The Throat chakra is also the area that links to responsibilities, and to taking charge of the direction of your life. To harmonize the energy flow to this chakra, or to remove a blockage, lie or sit comfortably in a peaceful room. Take hold of your sensitive aquamarine crystal and tune into its courageous energy, then place or hold it on your Throat chakra for 5 minutes. Close your eyes and give attention to your communication issues, sensing how your calming crystal is balancing and correcting the energetic vibrations here, then slowly come back into the room. Cleanse the stone (see pages 149–153). Benefit from this crystal energy daily for one or two weeks until you feel you can express yourself openly once more and say, from your heart, what you truly mean.

The Throat chakra and symbol

ALTERNATIVE COMMUNICATION CRYSTALS TO USE

Turquoise: aids creative communication, helps find ultimate purpose in life

Lapis lazuli: encourages taking charge of life, aids eloquent self-expression

Kyanite: promotes speaking the truth and clear communication

Improving your intuition with sodalite

Rough

Problem

If you are finding it hard to connect with your inner wisdom or if you have lost your ability to take command of situations, the energy in the middle of your forehead will be lacking.

Solution

To tap into your inner wisdom or your intuitive powers, use some crystal energy on your Third eye chakra: the sixth energy center (see page 57).

Boost your energy

The Third eye chakra is the place where you can develop your psychic abilities—it is connected with your dreams, self-respect, and insight. To boost or harmonize the energetic flow or remove a blockage, lie or sit in a quiet room. Hold your perceptive sodalite crystal and tune in to its spiritual vibrations. Place or hold it on your Third eye chakra for 5 minutes as you think about your depleted intuitive powers. Sense how your crystal is re-aligning your energies, then slowly come back into the room. Cleanse the stone (see pages 149–153). Use daily for one or two weeks until you start receiving inner messages and have more mental clarity about your life.

The Third eye chakra and symbol

CRYSTAL FACTS

CRYSTAL TO USE: sodalite, dark blue, blue/white variegated stone

AVAILABILITY: commonly available

QUALITIES OF STONE: brings clarity and truth, increases spiritual awareness, accesses higher parts of mind, helps you stand up to beliefs, releases guilt and fears, encourages rational and logical thinking

WORKING ON: Third eye chakra in the middle of the forehead

COLOR NEEDED BY CHAKRA: indigo

PARTS OF BODY AFFECTED BY CRYSTAL: pituitary and pineal glands, brainstem (medulla oblongata)

HEALTH BENEFITS: associated with balancing metabolism, lowering blood pressure, boosting the functioning of the lymphatic system, helping digestive problems, aiding endocrine system

WHERE TO PLACE THE CRYSTAL: hold to forehead

ALTERNATIVE INTUITIVE CRYSTALS TO USE

Aquamarine: clarifies perceptive abilities, stimulates intuition

Malachite: encourages self-expression, increases empathy and intuition

Moonstone: accesses information from subconscious, promotes intuition

Rough

CRYSTAL FACTS

CRYSTAL TO USE: snow quartz (white), also known as milky quartz and quartzite, can be crystalline form or pebble

AVAILABILITY: commonly available

QUALITIES OF STONE: helps you learn lessons, enhances spirituality, calms and balances, can purify and protect, can link to deep inner wisdom, raises spiritual energy to highest level

WORKING ON: Crown chakra on top of head

COLOR NEEDED BY CHAKRA: violet or white

PARTS OF BODY AFFECTED BY CRYSTAL: pineal gland, brain (cerebral cortex)

HEALTH BENEFITS: associated with boosting the immune system, can work on any condition, activates pineal and pituitary glands, enhances brain functions

WHERE TO PLACE THE CRYSTAL: hold to top of head

Accessing your spirituality with snow quartz

Problem

When you have lost your love for life, your spirit is down, or your artistic side is unfulfilled, the energy around the top of your head will be deficient.

Solution

To enhance your spiritual wisdom and your appreciation of the beautiful things in life, work with some crystal energy on your Crown chakra: the seventh energy center (see page 57).

Boost your energy

The Crown chakra is also the place which allows you to meditate more deeply, and show kindness and compassion to others. To open this chakra to a positive energy flow or to get rid of a blockage, lie or sit in a peaceful room and pick up your supportive milky quartz crystal and sense its tactful emanations. Close your eyes and place or hold your crystal on your Crown chakra for 5 minutes. Now concentrate on raising your spirit and your negative attitude to life, letting your gentle white crystal increase the energetic vibrations here, then slowly come back into the room. Cleanse the stone (see pages 149–153). Use this crystal daily for one or two weeks and notice how good everything looks once more and how much more in tune you feel with nature, your spirit, and your artistic side.

The Crown chakra and symbol

ALTERNATIVE SPIRITUAL CRYSTALS TO USE

Natural quartz: aids meditation, helps you realize life's possibilities

Amethyst: promotes spiritual awareness, removes negative feelings

Celestite: helps meditation, awakens spiritual desire

Cleansing your aura with amethyst

Cluster

Problem
You have had a demanding day with frustrating problems at work or children's tantrums at home, plus travel stress.

Solution
Clearing your aura of all the day's negativity can refresh your mind, body, and spirit.

Cleansing your energy
The purple color of the amethyst crystal is believed by healers to represent the merging of night and day. Its soothing, calming qualities are supposed to ease the physical conscious into unconscious: going from being awake to falling asleep. A powerful and protective crystal, it can cleanse your aura of any debris that you have picked up during the day. Stand upright in a quiet room and pick up your amethyst stone. Close your eyes and ask the crystal to remove any negativity and dissolve any unhealthy emotions from the day, replacing them with a higher spiritual vibration. Circle the stone all around your body: the front, back, and sides, feeling a wonderful warmth as your energetic field is fully restored, then slowly come back into the room. Cleanse the stone (see pages 149–153). Repeat daily.

What is the aura?
The aura is a subtle energy field that surrounds the physical body. It has several layers that constantly change color due to the light that our bodies absorb. The aura shows our emotional, mental, and spiritual wellbeing.

CRYSTAL FACTS
CRYSTAL TO USE: amethyst (purple/lavender) geode, cluster or single point

AVAILABILITY: commonly available

QUALITIES OF STONE: reduces stress and tension, inspires divine love, protects against psychic attack, dissolves negative environmental energies, rebalances spirit, increases intuition

WORKING ON: the aura

HEALTH BENEFITS: associated with increasing right brain activity and pineal and pituitary function, cleanses the blood, fights acne, neuralgia, and insomnia, balances endocrine system and metabolism, eases headaches and digestive problems

ALTERNATIVE AURA CLEANSING CRYSTALS TO USE

Fluorite: protects psychically, cleanses and balances aura (right: purple fluorite)

Rutilated quartz: heals energetic vibrations, cleanses and energizes aura (right: smoky quartz with rutiles, single terminator)

Polished

CRYSTAL FACTS

CRYSTAL TO USE: rhodochrosite (pink), banded

AVAILABILITY: commonly available

QUALITIES OF STONE: heals emotional wounds and upsets, inspires forgiveness, promotes acceptance of self, encourages self-expression, can bring in a soulmate, inspires unconditional love

HEALTH BENEFITS: purifies blood and kidneys, improves poor eyesight, aids spleen, heart, pancreas, and pituitary gland, invigorates the sexual organs

WHERE TO PLACE THE CRYSTAL: on your Heart chakra in the center of your chest

Attracting a soulmate with rhodochrosite

Rhodochrosite is a pink, passionate crystal that dares you to be adventurous. Just holding the stone, you feel the urge to seek change and bring about those things you truly want. Perhaps you are single and your heart's desire is for a soulmate to be your lover and best friend—someone with whom to share your hopes and dreams. Rhodochrosite is a powerful love crystal that vibrates at a higher level than rose quartz, so is very effective for removing any emotional blockages you have set up in your Heart chakra and increasing your sexual attraction. Legend also says that rubbing this vibrant crystal over your face improves your complexion, making you more beautiful and appealing to a new lover.

Crystal energizing

To attract your dream partner, have a quiet night at home and sit on your living room floor. Light two pink candles, as pink links to Venus, the goddess of love. Burn some sensual ylang ylang essential oil. Now write down on paper the characteristics of the partner you desire and fold it in four. Pick up your rhodochrosite crystal and hold it with your love list to your heart for about ten minutes. Close your eyes and visualize your new lover: see you both together, holding hands and laughing; feel your love and send this emotion flowing into this potent stone and out again for it to do its romantic work; and then slowly come back into the room. Repeat this love visualization regularly until your soulmate appears in your life.

ALTERNATIVE LOVE CRYSTALS TO USE

Rose quartz: purifies and opens the heart, attracts a new partner

Celestite: alleviates pain and brings in love

Increasing your sexuality with red tiger's eye

In the past, tiger's eye was believed to be "all-seeing" because of its banded appearance. A rich, earthy stone, natural tiger's eye is heat-treated to achieve the stone's deep red color.

Ruled by the bright sun, red tiger's eye is a supportive stone that lets you go inside to find the courage and confidence to resolve your sexual problems. In a long-term relationship it is common for sexual desire to wane, or a loss of interest in sex may be triggered by too much stress or a bout of depression. This bright, stimulating crystal matches the color needed by the sexual organs to stay healthy. The vibrational level of the stone stirs up the dormant sexual energies, curing any imbalances and reawakening your sexual desire.

Polished

Crystal cure

To rebalance your sexual organs and your root chakra, lie on your bed in late evening, placing your red tiger's eye on your lower pelvis for about ten minutes. Close your eyes and let the stone's energy correct any physical imbalances, and dissolve any emotional blockages such as self-criticism or a lack of self-worth. Open yourself up to the motivational healing and ask for a return of your sexual interest, then slowly come back into the room. Work nightly for a week until your emotional barriers melt and you feel the stirring of sexual desire once more.

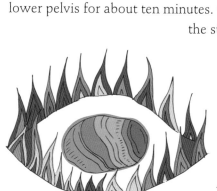

CRYSTAL FACTS

CRYSTAL TO USE: red tiger's eye (a form of quartz), banded can be small and tumbled

AVAILABILITY: commonly available

QUALITIES OF STONE: provides motivation, increases sex drive, balances emotions, enhances perceptions and insight; grounding and balancing

HEALTH BENEFITS: relieves asthma, aids the digestive system, balances spleen and pancreas, helps night vision, heals throat and reproductive organs

WHERE TO PLACE THE CRYSTAL: on your Root chakra in the lower pelvic area

ALTERNATIVE SEXUALITY CRYSTALS TO USE

Garnet: balances sex drive and reduces emotional upset

Fire agate: ignites sex drive, stimulates vitality

Ruby: fires up passion and enthusiasm for life once more

Healing a broken heart with agate

Polished

CRYSTAL FACTS

CRYSTAL TO USE: agate (clear/milky white, gray, green, pink, blue, brown), sometimes artificially colored, usually banded

AVAILABILITY: commonly available

QUALITIES OF STONE: gives strength and courage, improves ego and self-esteem, improves vitality, soothes and calms, promotes love, dissolves bitterness of the heart, helps with speaking the truth

HEALTH BENEFITS: stimulates digestive system, detoxes lymphatic system and pancreas, boosts circulatory system, reduces fevers, heals skin problems

WHERE TO PLACE THE CRYSTAL: over your Heart chakra or hold in hands

In past times, an agate was worn on the arm by gardeners to encourage fertility in their plants and crops. In today's world you can use the crystal's slow energy to encourage feelings of forgiveness and overcome the loss of a great love: the gentle energy of agate is ideal for healing a broken heart. The crystal gives first aid to the shell-shocked emotions, creating a safety net, and gradually bringing acceptance of what has happened. Recovering from the break-up of an intense love affair can be traumatic. Your world can fall apart and it can be hard to keep going. Your work, sleep, and eating patterns can all be disrupted in this emotionally depleting time. Agate is a wonderful emotional aid that can release your inner anger and kickstart your coping mechanism.

Crystal cure

A crystal that is often used in spells to draw in love, agate removes any spiteful tendencies you may be harboring toward an ex-lover. To heal your wounds, sit in a still room and pick up your agate stone. Close your eyes and really tune in to the stone's energy. Hold it in your hands or place on your heart in the middle of your chest and visualize your aching heart. Now see healing rays coming out from your stone and filling your heart, releasing the anger, pain, and sadness held there, making it whole once again. Feel your joy as the crystal fills your heart with love, then slowly come back into the room. Repeat several times to let go of grief. Cleanse the crystal well to keep it vibrant (see pages 149–153).

ALTERNATIVE LOVE-HEALING CRYSTALS TO USE

Chrysocolla: removes destructive emotions, works on heartache

Lavender (purple) jade: emotional balancer, dissolves upset and trauma

Kunzite: clears out deep-rooted hurts, heals heartache

Releasing a past lover with chrysocolla

Rough

A very tranquil stone, blue chrysocolla with its tiny flecks of copper looks similar to turquoise, and some people confuse the two. An emotional balancer, this crystal brings serenity and peace into the lives of people who have suffered heartache. A love affair may be long over and you may feel that you no longer care about your ex-partner, but often the ties with them can be so strong that it is hard to let go. Chrysocolla cleanses the Heart chakra of deeply held pain, sustaining you as your past emotional hurts are banished from your life.

CRYSTAL FACTS

CRYSTAL TO USE: chrysocolla (blue, turquoise, green), opaque

AVAILABILITY: commonly available

QUALITIES OF STONE: alleviates nervous tension, brings joy, enhances connection with inner self, aids meditation, heals heartache and inner child, can release negative emotions, reduces guilt

HEALTH BENEFITS: prevents ulcers, helps stomach problems caused by stress, helps PMS and period pains, treats eye problems and skin diseases, relieves arthritis, detoxifies liver and kidneys, and increases blood circulation

WHERE TO PLACE THE CRYSTAL: hold in hands

Crystal cure

To release your past lover, sit in a quiet room, close your eyes, and clasp your chrysocolla crystal in your hands. Visualize your ex-partner and see several golden cords connecting your hearts. Mentally pick up a pair of scissors and cut these cords, saying, "Thank you for your love but now I am releasing you from my life." See healing vibrations coming from your stone, and filling both your hearts with joy and anticipation for the new lovers in the future. Slowly come back into the room. Cleanse your crystal well (see pages 149–153).

ALTERNATIVE RELEASING CRYSTALS TO USE

Obsidian: cleanses the heart of old attachments and painful memories

Kunzite: heals the heart, disperses old, upsetting emotions

Aventurine: heals the heart, brings emotions back in control

Fostering commitment with opal

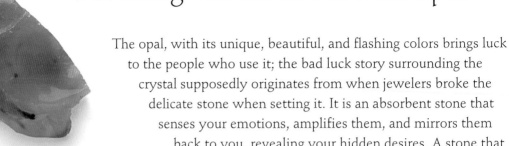

Rough

The opal, with its unique, beautiful, and flashing colors brings luck to the people who use it; the bad luck story surrounding the crystal supposedly originates from when jewelers broke the delicate stone when setting it. It is an absorbent stone that senses your emotions, amplifies them, and mirrors them back to you, revealing your hidden desires. A stone that teaches you to be responsible for your feelings, opal can show you how to resolve the emotional blockages that are preventing you from having a stable, long-lasting, and loving relationship. Commitment is a word that many people fear: you may have met the right partner but feel that he or she is not fully committing and that your relationship is stuck. Or it may be you who is holding back from finally binding yourself to that one person. The energy of a precious opal crystal can induce the loyalty and faithfulness you seek but beware of any doubts, as these can be amplified as well.

CRYSTAL FACTS

CRYSTAL TO USE: opal (white, black, beige, blue, yellow, brown, orange, red, purple, green, pink), milky appearance

AVAILABILITY: commonly available but gem opals can be expensive

QUALITIES OF STONE: balances emotions, controls temper, absorbs feelings, increases them and sends them back to source, brings loyalty and faithfulness, strengthens self-worth

HEALTH BENEFITS: aids eyesight, particularly as a gem essence, treats fever and infections, helps glandular dysfunction and fluid retention, reduces PMS

WHERE TO PLACE THE CRYSTAL: over your Heart chakra in the middle of your chest or hold in your hands

Crystal energizing

To encourage commitment from a partner or open up your heart, pick up your opal stone, close your eyes, and hold it in your hands or over your heart for several minutes while you visualize you and your partner together. See you both committing to each other. Feel how this shimmering crystal is intensifying your emotions and your partner's (it may well change color), releasing any fears, blockages, or inhibitions you both have about making a permanent relationship, then slowly come back into the room.

ALTERNATIVE COMMITMENT CRYSTALS TO USE

Garnet: encourages true love and emotional commitment

Magnetite: attracts love, long-term commitment, and a loyal partner

Rough

Making a positive relationship with green tourmaline

Green tourmaline is a delightful deep green; some forms show two or more colors when held to the light. The stone has many faces and can suit many moods, so it is no wonder that people say it has magical powers. A very fertile stone, it can stimulate growth in plants (see page 20), which you can replicate in the emotional side of your relationship.

Our relationships are often mirrors of our parents' marriage. Without awareness, we may be recreating the distant interaction that they had, and wonder why we are not happy. If there seems to be a wall of ice between you and your partner, a compassionate green tourmaline can give you the clarity to recognize what is causing your lack of intimacy, and help to bring your relationship back on track.

Crystal cure

Sit in a quiet room and hold the crystal to your heart. Closing your eyes, visualize both of you in a room ignoring each other: feel the tense emotions, then ask this nurturing stone to give you guidance and show you some way to resolve these feelings. Sense its healing rays surrounding you both and see how a positive solution to your communication problems pops into your head, then slowly come back into the room. Work daily with your crystal until you have a way to talk emotionally with your partner and to achieve the relationship you desire. Cleanse your crystal well (see pages 149–153).

CRYSTAL FACTS

CRYSTAL TO USE: green tourmaline, opaque/transparent, striated

AVAILABILITY: commonly available from specialist stores

QUALITIES OF STONE: brings in goodwill and friendship, dispels fear and negativity, balances emotions, restores enthusiasm and optimism, can help deal with problems constructively

HEALTH BENEFITS: aids sleep, balances the endocrine and nervous systems, boosts immune system, treats diarrhea and constipation, relieves migraines and asthma

WHERE TO PLACE THE CRYSTAL: hold on your Heart chakra in the middle of your chest

ALTERNATIVE RELATIONSHIP CRYSTALS TO USE

Turquoise: helps you to understand your partner

Opal: encourages you to become more emotionally responsive

Sugilite: dispels jealousy, fosters forgiveness and love

Rough

Banishing jealousy with sugilite

Sugilite is a very spiritual crystal that can cast light and love onto the blackest situations. Its alternative name is luvilite because it is a major love stone that opens the Heart chakra to unconditional love. Hostile or jealous feelings just do not survive around sugilite.

Jealousy in a relationship is a very destructive emotion. Some men, for example, can throw a jealous rage after seeing their partners just talking to another man. Women can be just as bad, secretly checking their partner's text messages or emails, if they mistrust them. Sugilite can transform these emotions before they threaten to destroy the relationship.

CRYSTAL FACTS

CRYSTAL TO USE: sugilite (also known as royal luvilite and royal azel—mauve-pink, purple, often with black manganese inclusions; lower grades are black with purple inclusions), opaque with bands, occasionally translucent, often tumbled

AVAILABILITY: available from specialist stores

QUALITIES OF STONE: an emotional balancer that relieves stress, gives spiritual awareness, brings love and wisdom, protects the inner self from emotional disappointments, disperses jealousy

HEALTH BENEFITS: increases functioning of the pineal, pituitary, and adrenal glands, balances brain hemispheres, removes toxins, clears headaches, and is good for pain relief

WHERE TO PLACE THE CRYSTAL: hold to Heart chakra in the center of the chest

Crystal cure

To cure jealous outbursts, you need to look inside yourself and realize that your partner is normally doing no wrong; it is your insecurities that are causing the jealousy. To change your emotional pattern, sit in a quiet room and pick up your sugilite crystal and place it on your heart. Think of your partner and ask the stone to help release your jealous inclinations. Feel this purple crystal's spiritual vibrations cleansing your heart of negative emotion, eliminating hostility and your possessive tendencies. Let it leave just pure love and tenderness for your partner. Work with the stone until your jealous tantrums cease. Cleanse it well to restore its vitality (see pages 149–153).

Polished

ALTERNATIVE HEALING CRYSTALS TO USE

Peridot: removes negative patterns, releases jealousy and resentment

Watermelon tourmaline: helps to resolve emotional conflict

Moving on a stale relationship with malachite

Working with the right crystal can give you the energetic shift to change a stale relationship into a positive one once more. Malachite is a powerful crystal that lets you express your true feelings. Many people believe it is a stone that attracts money into your life and emotionally it can attract feelings of love that you thought were lost. When you are in a relationship for several years it can become comfortable and settled but you often lose sight of the initial passion and excitement that were a major part of your first months together. Malachite is a transformational stone that wakes up old feelings, letting you feel that love again.

Crystal energizing

The high energetic level of malachite stirs your emotional depths to revitalize your stale relationship. Find a recent photograph of you and your partner, then sit in a dimly lit room holding your malachite crystal with the photograph in front of you. Look at your photograph and remember how you and your partner were in the early, heady days of your relationship. Experience, feel, and sense that initial excitement and sexual attraction. Now ask the crystal to help you recreate those initial feelings. Let its loving vibes inspire you to make some exciting changes with your partner to reawaken your latent passion for each other.

CRYSTAL FACTS

CRYSTAL TO USE: malachite (green), light and dark bands, can be tumbled or polished. Only use in polished form as the dust can be toxic

Rough

AVAILABILITY: commonly available

QUALITIES OF STONE: reduces stress and tension, cleanses the aura, removes spiritual blocks, increases hope and happiness, brings emotional balance and harmony, can be transforming

HEALTH BENEFITS: strengthens heart, boosts blood circulatory system and pineal and pituitary glands, aids sleep, relieves menstrual cramps, alleviates toothache, asthma, arthritis, and swollen joints

WHERE TO PLACE THE CRYSTAL: hold in hands. If you experience mild heart palpitations using malachite, remove and replace with rose quartz

Polished

ALTERNATIVE LOVE-REVIVING CRYSTALS TO USE

Rose quartz: opens up heart, restores harmony, brings change

Rhodonite: transmutes resentments, helps reconciliation in love partnerships

Opal: fosters love and desire, encourages positive emotions

Letting go of an unhappy relationship with aventurine

CRYSTAL FACTS

CRYSTAL TO USE: aventurine (green, red, blue, brown, peach/orange), opaque, contains shiny particles

AVAILABILITY: commonly available

QUALITIES OF STONE: relieves troubled emotions, stimulates creativity, attracts money, boosts intuition, promotes perception and decisiveness, encourages emotional recovery and living your own truth

HEALTH BENEFITS: reduces fever and joint inflammation, improves muscle tissue, equalizes blood pressure, lowers cholesterol, stimulates metabolism, alleviates migraines, helps treat skin diseases

WHERE TO PLACE THE CRYSTAL: hold to Heart chakra in middle of chest

Polished

Most aventurine bought today is green. It is a lovely healing crystal that works on attuning the mind, body, and spirit. The rough stone is dull on the surface but is speckled with pieces of hematite and mica that sparkle when you turn it in the light. In magic spells aventurine is worn to strengthen eyesight, but this ability also works spiritually, bringing a clearer insight into your current problems.

A stone that can calm troubled emotions, aventurine can give you the courage to end a relationship or marriage and cope with the sadness, and often bitter feelings that this separation brings. Making that final decision to split up because your love has died is traumatic and can be eased emotionally by this embracing savior that supports you in breaking away from a difficult and painful situation.

Crystal cure

Leaving an unhappy relationship, you can experience relief but also other complex emotions: fear, anger, betrayal, sorrow, or loneliness. To help you deal with these emotions, sit in a quiet room and pick up your aventurine crystal. Close your eyes and hold it to your heart, sensing each emotion you are experiencing, one by one. As each one surfaces, feel the crystal's responsive energy soothing and calming you and offering you a more empathetic way to handle your break up, then slowly come back into the room. Use for several days until you see a positive way forward. Cleanse the stone well (see pages 149–153).

ALTERNATIVE RELEASING CRYSTALS TO USE

Obsidian: dissolves love connections and heals barbs left in heart

Peridot: helps you let go of a relationship, eliminates negative patterns

Polished egg

CRYSTAL FACTS

CRYSTAL TO USE: green jade, translucent (jadeite) or creamy (nephrite)

AVAILABILITY: generally available but can be hard to find; nephrite is more easily available

QUALITIES OF STONE: balances emotions, calms the nervous system, releases negative thought patterns, encourages peace and unconditional love, creates inner harmony, releases irritability

HEALTH BENEFITS: strengthens heart and kidneys, removes toxins, eases bladder problems, improves eye disorders, aids fertility

WHERE TO PLACE THE CRYSTAL: hold in hands, and put by bed

Reducing bitter arguments with green jade

For thousands of years jade has been renowned in different cultures as a symbol of love, longevity, virtue, and wisdom: the superstitious Chinese wore bird images made from jade to protect and prolong their lives. The purity of the crystal soothes emotional upsets, dispelling any surrounding negativity.

Jade is also a supreme emotional balancer, taking the fire out of an argument, reducing the verbal ricochet. Arguing occasionally with a partner is a normal, healthy interaction between two personalities with different viewpoints, but constant heated arguments where cruel words are spoken can leave you both emotionally drained, damaging your feelings for each other.

Crystal cure

When you want to resolve the dysfunctional side of your relationship, jade can be your nurturing amulet and restore good communication. Take hold of your crystal and ask it to stop the senseless arguments and fill both you and your lover with unconditional love. Feel your joy as you experience this deep, intimate emotion. Cleanse the stone well (see pages 149–153) and place it by your bed so that it can carry on protecting you and promoting a harmonious relationship while you sleep.

ALTERNATIVE HARMONIZING CRYSTALS TO USE

Emerald: increases love and promotes a balanced relationship

Fluorite: stabilizes relationships, makes you understand emotional needs (right: green fluorite)

Increasing intuition with amethyst earrings

Purple is the color of royalty, and exquisite amethyst jewels have adorned crowns, rings, collars, and bracelets for centuries. A stone of great healing, amethyst aids meditation and increases your spiritual awareness and knowledge. Following your inner guidance helps you to make the right decisions in life. But when you are busy or living a hedonistic lifestyle you can ignore these "nudgings" or "messages" and come off your true life path. Amethyst can help you to connect with your sixth sense—your wisdom or intuition—once more.

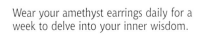

Wear your amethyst earrings daily for a week to delve into your inner wisdom.

Crystal energizing

When you start listening to your intuition, your mind and spirit merge and are in accord. Wearing purple amethyst earrings helps you become more in tune with your Third eye chakra: your inner vision center. In the past, earrings were worn less for their beauty and decorative appeal and more as protection to keep away negativity and disease from the ears. When you put on your amethyst earrings, sense how you merge with these spiritual crystals, feeling how their gentle emanations are calming your active mind, making you feel less distracted, and letting you hear your deepest emotional needs.

CRYSTAL FACTS

CRYSTAL TO USE: amethyst (purple/lavender), polished

WORKS ON: Third eye chakra in the middle of the forehead

COLOR OF CHAKRA: indigo

QUALITIES OF STONE: aids meditation, increases intuition and spirituality, reduces stress and tension, focuses decision-making, improves memory, increases motivation. Physically it heals acne and neuralgia, cleanses the blood, and releases the tension of headaches

DEITIES: Bacchus, Dionysus, Diana

SACRED TO: the ancient Greeks, who believed it could prevent drunkenness because of the legend surrounding Dionysus, the god of wine (see page 84). Jewish priests wore it to symbolize spiritual power

ASSOCIATED WITH: brainstem (medulla oblongata)

JEWELRY: cleanse regularly (see pages 149–153). Do not wear continuously for weeks on end as the effect can be too powerful

ALTERNATIVE CRYSTAL EARRINGS TO USE

Kyanite: brings compassion, stimulates intuition and psychic abilities

Azurite: cleanses the third eye, increases intuitive knowledge

Expressing yourself with sacred turquoise

A stone of spiritual self-expression, turquoise is sacred to many ancient religions and cultures, from ancient Egyptians to Tibetan Buddhists. This healing crystal is also associated with truth—"true blue" turquoise was once given to lovers for it signified that, if the stone faded, love faded too. Wearing turquoise can overcome a fear of public speaking. It also encourages you to tell the truth about what you want from others.

Wear turquoise every day for two weeks until you have released your speech inhibitions.

Crystal energizing

To let your inner voice and thoughts come through so that you can relate your emotions, wear a short turquoise pendant that hangs over your Throat chakra: your spiritual center of communication. To enhance the effectiveness of the crystal, wear turquoise earrings, as these will also work on the throat and help balance the energies in your head. A turquoise bracelet will stimulate the flow of energy in the body's meridians, encouraging you to express yourself well or to talk eloquently on your subject. The Navajo peoples use turquoise rings to guard against the evil eye, illness, and accidents, which may be why, traditionally, turquoise was said to be the travelers' or horsemen's stone. Riders wore it for protection, and often placed a tiny stone under their horse's saddle or on the bridle to safeguard their animals. You can use it when traveling too.

CRYSTAL FACTS

CRYSTAL TO USE: turquoise (blue), opaque, often veined

ASSOCIATED WITH: upper lungs and throat

WORKS ON: Throat chakra

COLOR OF CHAKRA: blue

QUALITIES OF STONE: enhances self-expression, releases inhibitions, dispels negativity, brings courage. Physically, has been worn to prevent migraines and calm the nervous system

DEITIES: the Great Spirit, Buddha, Hathor

SACRED TO: The Navajo peoples (as the stone of the Great Spirit); Buddhists; ancient Egyptians (Hathor was goddess of beauty, associated with Isis, queen of love and magic)

WEAR IT WITH: gold, its associated metal. Nepali Sherpa brides receive turquoise and gold jewelry as a wedding gift to bring marital happiness, luck, and prosperity

ALTERNATIVE CRYSTAL JEWELRY TO USE

Aquamarine: aids mental clarity, clears blocked communication, increasing self-expression

Lapis lazuli: teaches the importance of the spoken word, encourages self-awareness and speaking inner truth

Rose quartz for higher self-love

Rose quartz is the stone of joy and fulfillment. It will draw love to you whenever you need it, enhancing confidence and self-esteem, and bringing more magic and love to all your relationships. This crystal is also associated with deep healing; perhaps a much-loved partner has left, or your self-respect has been damaged.

CRYSTAL FACTS

CRYSTAL TO USE: rose quartz (pink), polished or rough

ASSOCIATED WITH: the heart and lower lungs

WORKS ON: Heart chakra in middle of your chest

COLOR OF CHAKRA: pink/green

QUALITIES OF STONE: purifies the heart, brings compassion, inner healing, and self-love; releases unexpressed emotions. Physically, detoxes the body

DEITY: the Great Mother

SACRED TO: shamans in many cultures; Wiccans

WEAR IT WITH: silver, copper, gold, its associated metals. Do not wear continuously for weeks—the effect can be too powerful

Crystal energizing

To increase self-love and loving emanations to your heart area, you need to wear a long rose quartz pendant that hangs over your Heart chakra, your spiritual energy center of love and compassion, in the center of your chest. If you can find heart-shaped rose quartz, this enhances the love vibrations. Focus on the healing for your heart, so that your rose quartz can carry the message to your inner self.

A love ritual

Rose quartz also promotes fidelity. If you have suffered hurt in your partnership, place a large healing rose quartz crystal by your bed. The Chinese used a variation, where a large rose quartz geode was placed under the left side of the bed (where the woman slept). This was sure to keep a man faithful.

Wear rose quartz every day for two to four weeks until your love energies are back to full strength.

ALTERNATIVE CRYSTAL PENDANTS TO USE

Emerald: balances internal feelings, enhances unconditional love, promoting friendship and partnership

Aventurine: boosts emotional healing and wellbeing, brings compassion and empathy

Balancing emotional disharmony with a garnet bracelet

In ancient times the deep red color of the garnet crystal was said to illuminate the night sky. It was believed that the crystal's rich color increased the heat of fire and brought healing and enlightenment. This purifying stone brings light into your life and heals a damaged spirit. It can show you the way out in a crisis, turning despair into a challenge after emotional outbursts with a partner at home or a work colleague.

Crystal healing

When your emotions are unstable you can feel very tired and drained. Putting on a fiery, red garnet bracelet grounds your Root chakra and improves your energetic flow. Even when your emotional problems seem insurmountable, this stone's powerful emissions increase your vigor, giving you the necessary courage to find solutions. A very protective stone, in the ancient past garnet was thought to keep away any ghosts or demons. As you put on your bracelet, notice how your ghosts start to leave, and feel you have the support and the confidence to handle anything.

Wear your garnet bracelet for several days until you feel more emotionally centered.

CRYSTAL FACTS

CRYSTAL TO USE: garnet (red), transparent or translucent, polished

ASSOCIATED WITH: lower pelvic area and adrenal glands

WORKS ON: affects Root chakra at bottom of spine and body's meridians

COLOR OF CHAKRA: red

QUALITIES OF STONE: stimulates love and compassion, increases imagination, encourages self-confidence and success, cleanses and re-energizes chakras, strengthens survival instinct. Physically it protects against infection, purifies the bloodstream, boosts the heart and lungs, and stimulates the metabolism

SACRED TO: Mayans; Aztecs

JEWELRY: cleanse regularly (see pages 149–153). Do not wear continuously for weeks as the effects can be too powerful

ALTERNATIVE CRYSTAL BRACELETS TO USE

Citrine: releases negative emotions, promotes joy in life

Rhodonite: emotional balancer, shows both sides of a problem

Taking control of your life with a jet necklace

Just like amber, jet is an unusual crystal that becomes electrically charged when it is rubbed. Choose carefully when buying jet as many pieces sold today are just black glass. A solid, glasslike dark crystal, jet has strong protective qualities and in the olden days was worn to protect against dark spirits. Today it can guard against unreasonable worries or fears: it evens out mood swings and can stop you feeling depressed. Jet can help in times when your life seems to spiral out of control with too many projects at work, or a demanding family to look after.

Crystal energizing

If you are starting to lose control, wearing a long jet necklace will help to harmonize the energy flow in your stressed meridians, allowing you to slow down and stabilize your emotions. Put on the necklace and sense how the crystal's properties are calming your nervous system and balancing your stress. Do not lend this stone to anyone as it is believed to become part of you, showing your personality.

Wear your jet necklace for several days
to get your life back on track.

CRYSTAL FACTS

CRYSTAL TO USE: jet (black), polished

ASSOCIATED WITH: all organs

WORKS ON: body's meridians

QUALITIES OF STONE: reduces fear and depressed feelings, protective, boosts psychic abilities, helps take control of life, emotional balancer, removes negative energy. Physically it can ease menstrual cramps, relieves stomach ache, and soothes the pain of migraines

DEITY: Cybele, the goddess of growth

SACRED TO: ancient Greeks who worshipped Cybele

JEWELRY: cleanse regularly (see pages 149–153). Do not wear continuously for weeks as the effects can be too powerful

ALTERNATIVE CRYSTAL JEWELRY TO USE

Sodalite: calms panic attacks, brings emotional balance and self-trust

Onyx: brings self-control and a more stable way of living

Following your spiritual path with blue sapphire earrings

An eye-catching, tranquil crystal, the blue sapphire is a wisdom stone that lets you seek your spiritual truth. It focuses and stills the mind, allowing you to dismiss unwanted thoughts. In today's world, it can be hard to stay on your spiritual path: your job may pay well but suppress your creativity, or you may have a partner who discourages spiritual develop-ment. The sapphire resolves any spiritual confusion, giving you the wisdom and confidence to make the right changes.

Wearing sapphire for up to one week can help illuminate your spiritual path.

CRYSTAL FACTS

CRYSTAL TO USE: blue sapphire, polished or cut

ASSOCIATED WITH: upper lungs, throat, thyroid, and parathyroid glands

WORKS ON: head energies and Throat chakra

COLOR OF CHAKRA: turquoise blue

QUALITIES OF STONE: inspires imagination and creativity, gives peace of mind, attracts friendship, love, and good luck, facilitates self-expression, develops psychic abilities. Physically it stimulates the pituitary gland and complete glandular system, soothes the eyes, and relieves insomnia

DEITIES: Apollo

SACRED TO: ancient Greeks who wore the stone when visiting oracles

JEWELRY: cleanse regularly (see pages 149–153). Do not wear continuously for weeks as the effects can be too powerful

Crystal energizing

Sapphire is known as the jewel of truth and clarity, the stone of destiny that helps you achieve your dreams. To open yourself up to your spiritual desires, wear blue sapphire earrings. The energetic impulse of this beautiful stone enhances your psychic abilities and opens your Throat chakra, your communication center, more fully, so that you express your needs. In magic spells a sapphire increased the potency of the spell or brought prosperity: use it to bring the spiritual abundance you are seeking.

ALTERNATIVE CRYSTAL EARRINGS TO USE

Agate: encourages quiet contemplation to stimulate spiritual growth (right: green moss agate)

Topaz: helps spiritual development, connects you to inner wisdom (right: golden topaz)

Overcoming mistakes with a snowflake obsidian ring

Wear your snowflake obsidian ring for several days to clear the negative events in your life.

This delightful black crystal with its whitish crystallite snowflakes is actually volcanic glass, formed when the lava cooled. A calming, soothing stone, snowflake obsidian is also called flowering obsidian; it helps you to recognize stressful mental attitudes and teaches you that life is a learning curve. Sometimes we have to make mistakes to gain experience from them. A failed business relationship, or course can linger on in our psyches as mistakes, and this crystal of change helps you release these distorted thought patterns.

CRYSTAL FACTS

CRYSTAL TO USE: snowflake obsidian (mottled black and white), polished

ASSOCIATED WITH: all organs

WORKS ON: body's meridians

QUALITIES OF STONE: absorbs and releases negativity, reduces mental stress, grounding, fosters inner wisdom and introspection, clears the mind of confusion, harmonizes mind, body, and spirit. Physically it aids the stomach and digestion, alleviates joint pain, helps arthritis, benefits the circulation of blood

DEITIES: Aztec—Tezcatlipoca ("smoking mirror" or "shining mirror")

JEWELRY: cleanse regularly (see pages 149–153). Do not wear continuously for weeks as the effects can be too powerful

Crystal energizing

When emotions relating to past events or mistakes need releasing from your subconscious, wear a snowflake obsidian ring on the ring finger (third from thumb) of your left hand. In the past this finger was believed to have special powers, and herbal medicines were often applied to the body using this finger. Rings were also considered sacred and magical as the ancient gods and goddesses wore them. To allow some magic into your life and increase your energetic flow, put the ring on your finger, and, mentally run through these events, sensing and feeling the special powers of this crystal turning them around so that you see their positive aspects.

ALTERNATIVE CRYSTAL RINGS TO USE

Peridot: helps to see mistakes, accept their guidance, and move on

Rhodonite: clears past emotional wounds, encourages self-esteem

Checking for physical illness with a pendulum

If your energetic field is blocked or lacks good energy flow (see page 57) you can eventually become ill. If you are suffering from confusing physical symptoms, or are unsure what organ is malfunctioning, you can diagnose the area that needs treating with a pendulum.

Crystal diagnosing

To use your pendulum, see page 19. A clockwise swing is normally "yes," although it can be opposite. "No" is generally counterclockwise. A side-to-side swinging movement indicates "don't know." Now sit in a quiet room and test your organs from your lower pelvis to your head. Hold the pendulum over each area and ask: "Are these organs healthy?" If you get a "no" or "don't know" response to an area of your body, treat it for 10 minutes daily for a week with a relevant crystal (see box) and seek medical advice. The color of the crystal resonates with the vibrations of the organ you are treating.

ORGANS AND CRYSTALS

Organs and glands	Color	Crystals
Lower pelvis—adrenals	red	red jasper, ruby, red tiger's eye
Pelvic area—kidneys, bladder, intestines, ovaries, gonads	orange	carnelian, amber, orange calcite
Below breastbone—spleen, stomach, liver, and pancreas	yellow	citrine, golden topaz, golden beryl (heliodor)
Middle of chest—lower lungs and heart	green (rose)	rose quartz, aventurine, chrysoprase
Middle of throat—upper lungs and throat, thymus	turquoise blue	turquoise, lapis lazuli, chrysocolla
Middle of forehead—brainstem, pituitary and pineal glands	indigo	amethyst, sodalite, azurite
Top of head—brain and pineal glands	violet (white)	clear quartz, lepidolite, violet fluorite

CRYSTAL FACTS

CRYSTAL TO USE: natural quartz pendulum with chain

AVAILABILITY: commonly available from crystal stores

QUALITIES OF STONE: receives, transmits, and amplifies energy, increases psychic abilities and intuition, dispels negativity

HEALTH BENEFITS: heals any condition, stimulates pineal and pituitary glands, relieves headache and toothache

WHERE TO PLACE THE CRYSTAL: move pendulum over body

HOW DOWSING WITH A PENDULUM WORKS: a natural quartz pendulum is a valuable diagnostic tool: allowing you to ask questions of your subconscious. Answers come through the electromagnetic energies emitted by your hand moving the pendulum

Curing headaches with amethyst

Cluster

CRYSTAL FACTS

CRYSTAL TO USE: amethyst (purple/lavender), geode, cluster or single point

AVAILABILITY: commonly available

QUALITIES OF STONE: ideal meditation crystal, increases psychic abilities, calms and protects, relieves stress and tension, lifts the spirit, gives mental focus, promotes spiritual wisdom

HEALTH BENEFITS: strengthens functioning of endocrine and immune systems, alleviates acne, neuralgia and insomnia, cleanses the blood, heals respiratory disease, eases headaches

WHERE TO PLACE THE CRYSTAL: hold to head

In Greek mythology a young maiden called Amethyst was turned into white quartz by Artemis, goddess of fertility, after Dionysus, god of wine, tried to kill her when he realized she didn't drink alcohol. Remorseful of his deed, Dionysus cried and dropped his wine goblet, and the flowing red wine ran over the quartz crystal turning it into the stone we know today as amethyst. Since then, the crystal has been renowned for its ability to cure hangovers.

Amethyst is a purifying and protective crystal. Its color, purple is associated with spirituality and brings inner vision and psychic awareness. Well known as a healer, many years ago amethyst was often rubbed into the face with saliva to heal pimples and flaky skin. It is also believed to be a great pain-reliever, and its calming vibrations may be used to relieve the constricting tension of headaches when the muscles and blood vessels around the scalp and neck tighten, bringing pain and discomfort.

Crystal healing

To reduce the pain of a headache, sit in a darkened room and pick up your amethyst crystal; clasp the stone tightly to connect to its healing properties. Now place the stone on the part of your head or neck that is painful for 5–10 minutes. Let the cool crystal soothe your pain. Cleanse it well after use (see pages 149–153). If your headaches are regular, do seek medical advice.

ALTERNATIVE TENSION-RELEASING CRYSTALS TO USE

Larimar: draws out pain, relieves constricted blood vessels

Magnesite: relaxes muscle tension, eases headaches

Smoky quartz: alleviates pain, reduces muscle restriction

Easing stomach ache with amber

Nicias, an ancient Greek, wrote in the 5th century BCE that amber was the essence of the setting sun, which had congealed in the sea and been cast up on the shore. This bright, sunny stone is not actually a crystal but a fossilized resin, first formed between 360 and one million years ago. As the resin oozed from pine trees, insects and plant material were trapped in the flow that fossilized into amber. In the past, beads of amber were often worn to prevent digestive problems as the stone is thought to be able to remove disease from the body, absorb pain, and let the body heal itself. Its yellowy orange color links to the unique vibrations of the stomach so it can ease the pain of stomach ache or an upset brought on by indigestion as a result of overeating or eating spicy foods.

Crystal healing

To soothe stomach pain, sit in a quiet room and hold the stone in your hands for a few minutes to sense its warming energies. Now place it on your stomach for about ten minutes, or until your pain subsides, as this cleansing stone clears the disturbance in your stomach and rebalances your body's energetic flow. Cleanse the stone after use to restore vitality (see pages 149–153). Do seek medical advice if symptoms persist, and/or are acute.

CRYSTAL FACTS

CRYSTAL TO USE: amber (yellow, orange, golden/ brown), transparent or opaque; some have insects or vegetation trapped inside, as it is actually a fossilized tree resin

AVAILABILITY: commonly available, but beware of imitations. One way to check if it is genuine is to make a saltwater solution with 1 tablespoon salt in a glass bowl of water and place the amber in it. If it floats it is amber, if it sinks it is artificial

QUALITIES OF STONE: encourages compassion, changes negative energy into positive, helps with depressive tendencies, inspires the intellect, aids self-expression, brings wisdom, can release pent-up emotions, helps to protect from radiation from sun, x-rays, and computers

HEALTH BENEFITS: boosts endocrine system, spleen, heart, liver, and bladder, reduces earache and asthma symptoms, gives vitality, helps to remove disease from body, treats throat problems, heals the stomach

WHERE TO PLACE THE CRYSTAL: hold to stomach

Polished

ALTERNATIVE STOMACH PAIN-RELIEVING CRYSTALS TO USE

Yellow jasper: releases toxins and eases stomach pain

Labradorite: regulates metabolism, heals stomach pain (right: polished egg)

Relieving PMS and menstrual cramps with moonstone

Rough

Sacred to all the lunar goddesses, moonstone is a beautiful, feminine, and loving crystal. As it links to the moon in the night sky, placing a crystal under your pillow is thought to bring blissful rest. Moonstone is also a fertility talisman, and in the Arab world women often sewed moonstones into their clothing to help them get pregnant. The crystal merges with the waxing and waning cycle of the moon, so is thought to have a balancing effect on the female menstrual cycle. Its calming energy may help ease the symptoms of premenstrual syndrome (PMS), such as irritability, depression, fatigue, a bloated stomach, and headache.

CRYSTAL FACTS

CRYSTAL TO USE: moonstone (white, cream, yellow, blue, brown, green) cloudy and translucent

AVAILABILITY: commonly available

QUALITIES OF STONE: balances emotions, reduces tendency to overreact, increases inner wisdom and clairvoyance, relieves anxiety, increases sensitivity, attracts happiness, removes old emotional patterns

HEALTH BENEFITS: reduces menstrual problems and PMS, lessens fluid retention, boosts lymphatic system, good for fertility and breastfeeding, detoxes the body, an essence can help insomnia

WHERE TO PLACE THE CRYSTAL: hold to pelvic region or wear as jewelry

Crystal healing

To lessen the effects of PMS, sit in a quiet room a week or so before your period is due and pick up your moonstone. Connect to its healing energies and hold it on your pelvis for about 10 minutes, feeling its delicate vibration evaporating any tension, tearfulness, or tiredness. Repeat daily for a week. If when your period starts you suffer from cramps, hold your stone to your pelvis. Close your eyes and visualize the pain leaving your body; keep the stone in position until you feel some relief. Cleanse the stone after treatment to keep it vibrant (see pages 149–153).

ALTERNATIVE PMS/CRAMP-RELIEVING CRYSTALS TO USE

Chrysocolla: alleviates menstrual cramps, treats PMS

Labradorite: balances hormone levels, improves PMS (right: rough labradorite)

Jet: balances mood swings, relieves menstrual cramps

Alleviating menopausal symptoms with citrine

Citrine deposits are becoming increasingly rare, and most citrine that is sold today was once amethyst, heat-treated to a high temperature to attain the stone's yellow color and vibration. Red tints on the stone distinguish it from the more lemony, natural citrine, although in natural citrine red tints can indicate the presence of hematite. A wonderful, sunny stone, citrine is a powerful cleanser and energizer, never needing cleansing itself. It protects the aura, the body's energy field, and in ancient times was carried as a protective stone against deadly snake venom. The inspiring yellow color of the crystal has the power to stimulate the intellect and improve memory and concentration. Physically the stone can also help even out the hormonal imbalances that cause some of the more unpleasant symptoms of the menopause. Drinking a revitalizing citrine essence can lessen the severity of hot flashes or night sweats, both symptoms that plague many menopausal women.

Cluster

CRYSTAL FACTS

CRYSTAL TO USE: citrine (yellow, yellow/brown), often a geode point or cluster

AVAILABILITY: natural citrine can be hard to find; citrine produced by heat-treating amethyst is commonly available

QUALITIES OF STONE: lifts self-esteem, warms and energizes, brings hope, controls emotions, clarifies mental processes, improves memory, cleanses chakras, a beneficial stone linked to abundance

HEALTH BENEFITS: aids tissue regeneration, improves circulation, lessens anxiety and depression, alleviates digestive problems, helps heal kidney and bladder infections, works on hormonal and menopausal symptoms

WHERE TO PLACE THE CRYSTAL: make a gem essence

Crystal healing

Make your gem essence by rinsing the citrine under running water and placing it in a glass container or jar. Fill with still mineral water to cover the stone. Cover and place on a sunny table or windowsill for 1 or 2 hours or longer. Strain some of the liquid into a glass, keeping the rest. Drink the essence when you are feeling low or suffering a hot flash and feel how the crystal starts to lower your temperature and lift your mood. Drink whenever needed.

ALTERNATIVE MENOPAUSE-RELIEVING CRYSTALS TO USE

Lepidolite: relieves exhaustion, aids menopausal symptoms

Blue tourmaline: relieves distressing menopausal night sweats

Helping backache with rutilated quartz

Rutilated quartz is an attractive clear crystal with colorful golden rutile, copper, or blue titanium fibers that glow in the light. Like all quartzes it is a powerful healing stone that amplifies energy flow. In physical ailments it is thought to detoxify the blood of waste products, and stimulate the body's innate healing force, reducing inflammation caused by damaged back muscles—from an accident or postural problems. The crystal can also encourage the regeneration of body tissue, speeding up healing.

CRYSTAL FACTS

CRYSTAL TO USE: rutilated quartz (milky with silver, gold, copper-colored, brown, red, or black strands), also known as angel hair

AVAILABILITY: commonly available

QUALITIES OF STONE: alleviates depression, helps inspiration, soothes dark moods, aids transition

HEALTH BENEFITS: regenerates cells and repairs damaged body tissue, boosts immune system, helps chronic pain

WHERE TO PLACE THE CRYSTAL: hold it on the painful area of your back

Cut and polished

Crystal healing

If you suffer a painful attack of back pain, lie flat on your bed and place your rutilated quartz crystal under the painful area for about 15 minutes, letting the crystal's strong energy focus on dissipating the pain and encourage healing in the inflamed tissues, muscles, or discs. Someone can also work on the pain by circling the crystal clockwise over the affected area for 15 minutes, "pulling" out the negative energy. Use the crystal regularly until the pain goes. Cleanse it well to keep vibrant (see pages 149–153).

ALTERNATIVE BACKACHE-RELIEVING CRYSTALS TO USE

Magnetite: acts as an antispasmodic and relaxes muscles

Fire opal: re-energizes, its vibrations relieve pain in lower back

Smoky quartz: alleviates pain, strengthens back muscles (right: polished)

Soothing physical pain with carnelian

Polished

CRYSTAL FACTS

CRYSTAL TO USE: carnelian

AVAILABILITY: commonly available

QUALITIES OF STONE: energizes and aids motivation and mental focus, releases negative patterns

HEALTH BENEFITS: increases fertility, helps tissue regeneration, treats sores, muscular spasms, and wounds, treats rheumatism and arthritis

WHERE TO PLACE THE CRYSTAL: hold it on affected area

The word carnelian, or cornelian, may be derived from the Latin word *carne*, which means "flesh," a reference to the orangey red coloring of the stone, which is caused by the presence of iron oxides. This high-energy stone is believed to be particularly good at removing blockages and neutralizing the pain associated with ailments such as neuralgia, fever, infection, and muscular pain, and also treating nosebleeds.

Physical pain is the result of special sensory nerve endings being stimulated and sending pain messages to the brain because of bodily injury or disease. Energetically, a blockage, an excess of energy, or an imbalance in the body's energy channels (meridians) causes the physical pain that you feel, and all energy blockages need to be removed or harmonized to restore health and wellbeing.

Crystal healing

If you experience a nagging pain that does not seem to want to go away, you can help to remove the discomfort by using a carnelian crystal. Place the stone on or over the source of your pain for about 15 minutes to let the crystal do its work. As the throbbing pain begins to improve, remove the stone and cleanse it well (see pages 149–153).

ALTERNATIVE PAIN-RELIEVING CRYSTALS TO USE

Lapis lazuli: gentle pain reliever, helps headaches, boosts immune system

Blue calcite: dissolves pains, soothes pain, and removes anxiety

Magnetite: removes blockages, is anti-inflammatory, helps muscle strain or painful cramps

Treating colds and flu with fluorite

Polished

Many healers call fluorite the "genius" stone, as they believe it opens new pathways for the mind. As it is such a tactile and spiritual stone, communing with it can bring ideas from the spirit world into our own reality. Physically, using a green fluorite crystal, or drinking a crystal essence, can relieve nasty cold symptoms such as runny nose or sore throat, or can reduce the fever, aching muscles, and debilitating fatigue of the flu virus. It is believed that the crystal draws any negativity from the body, clearing the virus. A wonderful healing color, the green of the stone is also thought to encourage tissue and cell growth, while generally restoring body health.

Crystal healing

Sit in a quiet room and hold your crystal in your hands and feel its medicinal pulsations.

For a cold, place the stone over your nose for 5 minutes and then on your forehead for the same time, letting the stone fight the virus and clear congestion. For flu, hold the stone to your chest for 10 minutes, and sense the crystal's vibrations lowering your fever. Alternatively, drink a fluorite crystal essence (see page 16). Use the stone every few hours until you feel better, then cleanse it well (see pages 149–153).

CRYSTAL FACTS

CRYSTAL TO USE: green fluorite, transparent

AVAILABILITY: commonly available

QUALITIES OF STONE: protective psychic stone, increases concentration, aids meditation, grounds energy, helps to focus mind and store information, cleanses aura, boosts self-confidence, clears emotional trauma

HEALTH BENEFITS: reduces dental disease, relieves pneumonia, helps viral infection, reduces inflammation, strengthens teeth and bones and cells, reduces body toxins, relieves stomach disorders, alleviates arthritis and rheumatism

WHERE TO PLACE THE CRYSTAL: hold to nose, head, or chest, or use as essence

ALTERNATIVE COLD/FLU-RELIEVING CRYSTALS TO USE

Moss agate: boosts immune system, treats infection, lowers fever

Jet: relieves aches and pains, reduces cold symptoms

Helping eczema with blue calcite

Blue calcite is a very cleansing crystal that can absorb any negative vibrations that have become "stuck" in the physical body or the aura (our energetic field). Often used in purification ceremonies to add a brightness to the atmosphere, calcite can remove any lingering stagnancy from the environment. A well-known pain reliever, the crystal can be used to soothe the sore red skin and the itching sensations of eczema. Its healing rays are believed to cool hot and inflamed skin and act as a natural antiseptic.

Rough

Crystal healing

To ease your eczema, sit in a quiet room and pick up your blue calcite crystal and tune in to its cleansing qualities. Place or hold the stone over your irritated skin for about 5 minutes each time. You may feel a slight tingling as this gentle crystal works on relieving the pain and healing the affected skin tissue. Alternatively, make a calcite essence (to make, see page 16) and dab it on the skin. Repeat every few hours until you feel the itchy sensations abating. Cleanse the stone regularly to revitalize its energies (see pages 149–153).

CRYSTAL FACTS

CRYSTAL TO USE: blue calcite, translucent, waxy texture, can be banded (may be treated with acid to increase color)

AVAILABILITY: commonly available

QUALITIES OF STONE: reduces stress and fear, balances emotions, inspires joy, speeds up spiritual development, cleanses negative energies, increases spiritual development, soothes nerves, calms anxieties

HEALTH BENEFITS: lowers blood pressure, heals back pain, alleviates skin conditions, aids kidneys, pancreas, and spleen, helps to strengthen skeleton and joints, boosts immune system

WHERE TO PLACE THE CRYSTAL: hold to affected area or use as essence

Rough

ALTERNATIVE SKIN PAIN-RELIEVING CRYSTALS TO USE

Brown jasper: reduces inflammation, treats skin disorders

Moonstone: alleviates eruptions, relieves stress (right: opaque polished moonstone)

Relieving earache with rose quartz

Polished

CRYSTAL FACTS

CRYSTAL TO USE: rose quartz (pink), translucent, sometimes tumbled

AVAILABILITY: commonly available

QUALITIES OF STONE: can clear resentment, anger, guilt, or fear, relieves emotional trauma, opens you up to beauty, promotes romantic love, increases empathy and a sensitive attitude, supreme healer of pain

HEALTH BENEFITS: benefits the kidneys and circulatory system, increases fertility, releases waste products, soothes headaches, migraines, sore throat, earache, and burns, improves the complexion

WHERE TO PLACE THE CRYSTAL: hold to ear

The healing rays of rose quartz envelop the body like a soothing, cozy blanket. Emotionally this stone brings peace and forgiveness after heartbreak, a reminder that we can be happy and make our dreams come true. This lovely pink stone is also known as the children's stone, because it is thought to be effective at healing the childhood ailments and upsets that may follow us into adulthood. Earache, caused by an infection of the inner ear, is one childhood ailment which as adults we may also suffer from. The healing vibration of rose quartz is believed to help to fight the infection and give comforting pain relief.

Crystal healing

To reduce the pain of earache, place your rose quartz crystal in a warm towel and hold it to your ear or your child's ear for about 10 minutes. Alternatively, put it inside the cover of a hot water bottle filled with warm water and hold it to the ear. Feel how the gentle emissions of

this beautiful, compassionate stone are penetrating deep into the inner ear and reducing your pain. Work with the stone every few hours until the pain starts to diminish, then cleanse it well to keep it vibrant (see pages 149–151). Do consult a medical professional if symptoms continue or are acute.

ALTERNATIVE PAIN-RELIEVING CRYSTALS TO USE

Amber: can draw illness out of the body, absorbs pain of earache

Celestite: heals ear disorders, eliminates pain

Blue fluorite: amplifies healing potential, good pain relief for ear problems (right: green/blue purple banded fluorite)

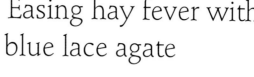

Easing hay fever with blue lace agate

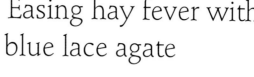

Rough

It is hard to feel anxious around blue lace agate. This serene crystal resonates peace and calm. In ancient home rituals, the stone was placed between two lit blue candles to reduce stress and quarrels and bring a harmonious atmosphere. The stone has a particular affinity with the Throat chakra, releasing any anger or unease that may have blocked communication, letting you calmly express your feelings. Physically, the cooling blue vibes of the gem can cool the heat of fevers. With allergic ailments, such as hay fever, it is thought to appease immune system reactions to pollen or molds, soothing irritating sneezing, itchy eyes, and nasal congestion. Using this crystal may also help when you don't have your regular remedy to hand.

CRYSTAL FACTS

CRYSTAL TO USE: blue lace agate, has white and light blue lines, banded, can be tumbled

AVAILABILITY: commonly available

QUALITIES OF STONE: helps to express thoughts and feelings, releases fears of rejection and repression, relieves stress and tension, works on Throat chakra to release blockages, neutralizes anger, and brings peace

HEALTH BENEFITS: heals throat infections, reduces inflammation and fevers, treats arthritis and bone problems, relieves shoulder and neck problems

WHERE TO PLACE THE CRYSTAL: hold to nose and face

Polished

Crystal healing

To ease hay fever symptoms, sit in a quiet room and pick up your blue agate. Hold it, connecting with its peaceful and tranquil energy. Hold the stone over your nose for about 5 minutes, letting its therapeutic emissions work on your inflamed nasal passages. Now move the crystal to your sinuses either side of your nose and hold for a few minutes on each side so that the stone's cooling energy eases the congestion and relieves your eyes. Use the crystal daily in the hay fever season, cleansing it after each session (see pages 149–153).

ALTERNATIVE HAY FEVER-RELIEVING CRYSTALS

Aquamarine: balances the reactions of the immune system in hay fever

Moss agate: an anti-inflammatory stone that boosts the immune system

Sodalite: increases functioning of immune system

Polished

Alleviating toothache with aquamarine essence

Aquamarine has a gentle and compassionate energy, and its beautiful light blue color resonates with the sea. Many legends surround this connection. One says that the stone was found hidden in the treasure chest of a mermaid.

Aquamarine's curative powers make it a lucky charm for the wearer who wants to stay healthy. Well known for stimulating and cleansing the Throat chakra, its cool energy can treat the irritation of a sore throat and swollen glands. The healing blue rays of the stone also resonate at the same rate as healthy cells in the jaw, so can correct the vibrational level of the damaged cells that are causing the dull throbbing pain or sharp twinges of toothache. When you have an interminable wait to see your dentist, an aquamarine remedy may help.

Crystal healing

Rinsing your mouth with a curative aquamarine essence (see also page 16) may reduce pain and soothe any gum inflammation that accompanies tooth decay, a fracture in the tooth, or an abscess. It can also strengthen your immune system so that your body rallies to fight the infection. To make the essence, rinse your aquamarine crystal under running water, then place in a glass container or a jar and fill with still mineral water. Cover and leave on a table or windowsill in the sun for about 1–2 hours, or leave this stone in moonlight for 3 hours; the longer you leave the essence the more potent it will be. Strain some liquid into a glass; reserve the rest. Wash the liquid around your mouth and over your affected tooth, feeling how this cleansing essence is reducing your acute twinges of pain. Repeat every 2 hours.

CRYSTAL FACTS

Crystal to use: aquamarine (green/blue), clear and opaque, faceted, can be small and tumbled

Availability: commonly available

Qualities of stone: clears the mind, sharpens the intellect, lessens fears, helps creative self-expression, brings peace and calm, protects the aura, increases intuition

Health benefits: strengthens kidneys, liver, spleen and thyroid, relieves throat and stomach troubles, soothes toothache, eases fluid retention, can help hay fever

How to use the crystal: make a crystal essence with it

ALTERNATIVE TOOTH-PAIN CRYSTALS TO USE

Amber: draws disease from the body, eases tooth pain

Lapis lazuli: great pain reliever, helps tooth discomfort and boosts immune system

Fluorite: powerful healer, regenerates gums, strengthens tooth (right: purple fluorite)

Soothing joint pain with rhodonite

Polished

Rhodonite is a peaceful and joyful pink crystal that opens up the Heart chakra to unconditional love. A "rescue" stone, it can ward off negative influences, raise self-worth and cleanse you of any limiting doubts you may have. Deeply rooted emotions can hold us back: rhodonite releases old fears or stubborn pride, emotions often held in the joints, which may manifest physically as a joint sprain, a damaged joint capsule, or the loss of protective cartilage associated with arthritis. The nurturing pink vibrations of the crystal can give some relief to the joint pain and encourage the growth of new, healthy bone and cartilage.

Crystal healing

To reduce the swelling of a painful joint injury or inflamed arthritic joints, take your compassionate crystal in your hands and feel a tingling as you sense its healing powers. Sit down comfortably and place the stone on your painful joint, or even tape it in position. Leave for 10–15 minutes. You may feel a

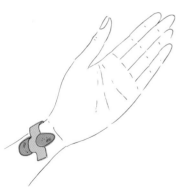

slight warmth as the crystal works on releasing any fear or inflexibility held in the joint, while also reducing the heat of the existing inflammation or injury. Repeat every day for a week or until you see some improvement. Cleanse your stone daily (see pages 149–153).

CRYSTAL FACTS

CRYSTAL TO USE: rhodonite (pink), mottled effect, often has flecks of black, can be tumbled

AVAILABILITY: commonly available

QUALITIES OF STONE: improves memory, reduces emotional trauma, lowers stress and calms the mind, raises self-esteem, clears out painful emotion, encourages forgiveness

HEALTH BENEFITS: balances central nervous system, improves hearing, heals wounds, aids bone growth, reduces joint inflammation and arthritic pain, can be drunk as an essence for shock or trauma

WHERE TO PLACE THE CRYSTAL: on the affected joint

ALTERNATIVE JOINT-HEALING CRYSTALS TO USE

Malachite: reduces swelling in joints, treats arthritis (use polished stone)

Obsidian: detoxifies and reduces joint pain, relieves arthritic discomfort

Fluorite: helps to mobilize joint, gives pain relief, and treats arthritis (right: green fluorite)

Soothing a sore throat with beryl

Today beryl is associated with helping to ease a sore throat; historically, it was prized as a stone of the voice and for eloquence, yet may, equally, be used as a shield to protect against heavy persuasion or a hard sell. Some people use this crystal to help them find an item that they have lost, just as a crystal essence made with beryl may treat a sore throat, perhaps helping you to recover your lost voice.

Polished

Crystal healing

If you have a sore throat you can treat it with a crystal essence (see also page 16) made with water and a beryl crystal. This potent crystal is associated with increasing your immunity to toxins and pollutants and works on the invading infection.

A crystal essence is easy to make. Rinse your beryl crystal under running water then place it in a glass container or jar. Fill with still mineral water until the stone is covered. Cover and place on a table or windowsill to be bathed in sunlight. Ideally leave for 1–12 hours: the longer you leave it, the stronger the essence. Strain some of the liquid from the stone into a glass; keep the rest. Add half a teaspoon of sea salt, which acts as a natural antiseptic. Gargle briefly and repeat every 2 hours until you feel the crystal's potency helping your throat to feel better.

CRYSTAL FACTS

CRYSTAL TO USE: beryl (pink, golden, yellow, green, white, blue) can be transparent and pyramid shape

AVAILABILITY: commonly available

QUALITIES OF STONE: reduces stress, increases willpower, helps in realizing potential, relaxes the mind

HEALTH BENEFITS: helps heart problems and liver upsets, treats stomach and throat infections, strengthens circulatory system

HOW TO USE THE CRYSTAL: make a crystal essence by soaking the stone in mineral water

ALTERNATIVE THROAT-RELIEVING CRYSTALS TO USE

Blue lace agate: reduces fever and fights throat and lymph infections

Aquamarine: great tonic, relieves sore throat and swollen glands

Improving immune system function with turquoise

Rough

Turquoise is a very supportive and strengthening crystal that is thought to give protection against environmental pollution and viral infections, and aid tissue regeneration. When we work too hard, eat unhealthily, and do not get enough sleep our immune system can become compromised, so it is vital to keep it healthy and functioning at its best.

Prized by ancient cultures, turquoise is regarded as sacred to some shamans because of its powerful healing ability. In healing visualizations, turquoise is believed to "absorb" the illness from the patient. It's also a symbol of prosperity, luck, and loyalty.

CRYSTAL FACTS

CRYSTAL TO USE: turquoise (blue), normally veined, often polished

AVAILABILITY: commonly available

QUALITIES OF STONE: aids intuition and creative thoughts, enhances communication, removes negative energy

HEALTH BENEFITS: strengthens entire body, boosts immune system, helps body to take in nutrients, helps tissue renewal

WHERE TO PLACE THE CRYSTAL: around the chest area

Crystal healing

If you are starting to feel run down, don't wait until you catch a cold or get the flu before you pay attention to the needs of your immune system. Take your crystal in your hand and connect with its healing energies, then ask it to keep you strong and free from illness. Slowly move it in clockwise circles for a few minutes around your chest area, feeling its positive emanations boosting your immunity to infection. Repeat daily to keep you well.

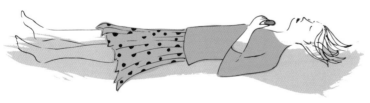

ALTERNATIVE IMMUNE-BOOSTING CRYSTALS TO USE

Moss agate: encourages removal of waste products, enhances immune system

Snow quartz: stimulates immune system, balances body

Brown jasper: clears toxins, strengthens immune system

Reducing travel sickness with yellow jasper

Jasper is available in a variety of colors. Yellow jasper occurs when the crystal is mixed with goethite, a yellow mineral of hydrated iron oxide. A powerful healer, it sustains the body during times of stress, giving the courage to attack problems head on.

Back in ancient Egypt, King Nechepsus always wore green jasper engraved with a dragon surrounded by rays to strengthen his digestive tract, and today jasper's curative properties are still used to strengthen digestion. Yellow jasper, in particular, may treat the discomfort of stomach upsets, and can relieve the nausea and vomiting of travel sickness. It may also stabilize the organ of balance in the inner ear, which gets disrupted by travel motion, bringing on the unpleasant queasy feelings.

Polished

Crystal healing

In the past jasper was worn as an amulet to keep away illness, so keep travel sickness at bay by taking out your jasper at the start of your journey. Hold it for about 5 minutes on each inner ear, then move it to your stomach for a further 10 minutes, feeling how this grounding, centered stone is balancing the function-ing of the organs in these areas and making you feel better. Keep moving the crystal between your ears and stomach for the rest of the journey. Cleanse it well after treatment (see pages 149–153).

CRYSTAL FACTS

CRYSTAL TO USE: yellow jasper, an opaque variety of chalcedony, can be patterned, sometimes water-worn, can be small and tumbled

AVAILABILITY: commonly available

QUALITIES OF STONE: nurturing stone that supports during stress, absorbs negative energies, clears environmental pollution, inspires imagination, and promotes clear thinking

HEALTH BENEFITS: boosts endocrine system, strengthens kidneys and liver, protects when traveling, alleviates stomach problems, soothes travel sickness or bilious attacks, releases toxins

WHERE TO PLACE THE CRYSTAL: hold it to ears and stomach

ALTERNATIVE SICKNESS-RELIEVING CRYSTALS TO USE

Malachite: reduces stomach cramps, helps travel sickness

Aventurine: a comforting stone; green aventurine is particularly good for settling nausea

Green fluorite: aids stomach upsets, reduces anxiety

Helping muscle cramps with hematite

Hematite is known as a protective crystal that grounds and balances the flow of environmental energies around the home (see page 12) but it is also a profound physical healer. Strongly connected to the blood and circulatory system, the stone appears to "bleed," producing a red line if you try to draw with it. Healers believe that hematite possesses special magical powers, spiriting away illness when placed on the body. This innate power can also work on muscle cramps: those short, painful spasms brought on by the contraction of muscle fibres. These spasms often happen immediately after a workout at the gym because lactic acid builds up in the muscles. Repetitive movement or lying in a fixed position for a long time can also bring cramps on.

Polished

CRYSTAL FACTS

CRYSTAL TO USE: hematite (silver/gray metallic when polished, reddish brown when rough)

AVAILABILITY: commonly available

QUALITIES OF STONE: enhances vitality and optimism, increases courage, boosts self-esteem and confidence, gives focus, takes away any self-limitations

HEALTH BENEFITS: stimulates circulatory system, helps insomnia, stimulates the spleen, aids fractures, alleviates leg cramps and stress and anxiety

WHERE TO PLACE THE CRYSTAL: hold it to affected muscle

Crystal healing

If you are prone to muscle cramps it is best to keep your hematite crystal with you at all times. This stone will increase the blood flow in the body, releasing the tightness and restriction in the muscles. When you feel a spasm starting, hold the crystal in your hand and ask for its help in removing the tension. Now place it on the affected muscle, wrapping your hands around the stone for about 5–10 minutes. Feel the crystal's restorative vibrations easing the pain and lessening the contraction. Cleanse it well after use (see pages 149–153).

ALTERNATIVE CRAMP-RELEASING CRYSTALS TO USE

Chrysocolla: strengthens blood and muscles, alleviates spasms or cramp

Amazonite: dissolves blockages in nervous system, relieves muscle cramps

Letting go of your stress with amethyst

Cluster

CRYSTAL FACTS

CRYSTAL TO USE: amethyst (purple/lavender) geode, cluster or single point

AVAILABILITY: commonly available

QUALITIES OF STONE: calms nervous system, heals emotions, relieves tension and stress symptoms

HEALTH BENEFITS: good blood cleanser, eases headaches, heals lung and digestive problems

WHERE TO PLACE THE CRYSTAL: on your forehead or stomach

Amethyst is the perfect crystal to instill peace and calm. A mind-protector, the stone increases vigor, deflecting any psychic attacks that may be aimed at you. Many peoples and cultures appreciated amethyst's qualities. During the Middle Ages, its soothing properties were adopted by the clergy, with both priests and cardinals wearing amethyst rings to symbolize their piety and celibacy.

Many healers deem amethyst to be "nature's tranquilizer" for its ability to relax the mind and destress the nervous system. Stress can be brought on by endless work pressures and deadlines, unemployment or relationship difficulties for example. Although a certain amount of stress is good for you, if it becomes long-term and your body is on constant "fight-or-flight" alert, burn-out can become a problem.

Crystal healing

An effective way of dealing with stressful situations is to use an amethyst to calm your body and emotions. Sit in a quiet place where you will not be disturbed and hold the stone to your forehead for about 5–10 minutes; or, if you are in a public place and prefer to use the stone more discreetly, just hold it in your hand. Feel the stone's calming vibrations releasing the stress from your body and slowing down your nervous system. Work with this crystal whenever your stress levels start to soar, and remember to cleanse it regularly (see pages 149–153).

ALTERNATIVE STRESS-RELIEVING CRYSTALS TO USE

Aquamarine: reduces stress, clears communication problems

Lapis lazuli: releases stress and brings inner peace

Lavender (purple) jade: regulates heartbeat, calms the nervous system, soothes the mind, alleviates anxiety

Calming your anger with agate

Rough

Agate is a powerful emotional healer that works slowly on taking away your inner bitterness and angry feelings. In ancient times, the crystal was highly valued as an amulet to quench the thirst and to soothe a fever. Today, agate can work on emotional upsets, taking the heat out of an upsetting argument and throwing "water" on overheated emotions.

Losing your temper in a business meeting or when your children are being disobedient in a public place just draws attention to yourself. Releasing angry feelings is important, because if they stay pent-up inside, you can become bitter and repressed. Working with a crystal can help you to express your feelings before you get to boiling point.

CRYSTAL FACTS

CRYSTAL TO USE: agate (clear/milky white, gray, blue, green, pink, or brown) translucent, usually banded

AVAILABILITY: commonly available, occasionally artificially colored

QUALITIES OF STONE: removes bitter anger and transforms negativity, grounds emotions

HEALTH BENEFITS: stimulates digestion and soothes stomach, releases toxins, heals skin disorders

WHERE TO PLACE THE CRYSTAL: hold in your hands

Crystal healing

When you feel an angry outburst about to surface, use your agate to calm your emotions—keep the crystal with you at all times. When you start to get angry, take hold of the crystal and and hold it in your hands for about 5 minutes, breathing deeply as the crystal starts to soothe your anger. Use this technique whenever you feel you may completely lose control.

ALTERNATIVE ANGER-RELEASING CRYSTALS TO USE

Moonstone: soothes emotional overreaction

Red garnet: reduces unreasonable anger, particularly toward yourself; turns a crisis into a challenge

Dealing with fear with natural quartz cluster

Cluster

CRYSTAL FACTS

CRYSTAL TO USE: natural quartz cluster (clear)

AVAILABILITY: commonly available

QUALITIES OF STONE: powerful healer and energy amplifier, tunes in to vibrational energy, lets you find spiritual purpose, aids concentration, fuels memory, purifies the soul

HEALTH BENEFITS: heals all conditions, relieves pain, aids diarrhea, soothes headaches, boosts immune system, soothes burns

WHERE TO PLACE THE CRYSTAL: solar plexus in upper abdomen

A natural quartz cluster is a beautiful clear crystal that looks like a piece of chiseled ice. The more you stare into the stone, the more you are supposed to see in it. Many ancient civilizations revered the crystal, using its high energetic vibration to increase the effectiveness of their religious and magical ceremonies. The ancient Japanese who worshiped the fiery dragon believed in the purity of quartz, thinking it was formed from a white dragon's breath.

Natural quartz heals the mind and spirit and can alter fixed mental attitudes, particularly fears. Fears can hold you back in life. Everyone experiences fears: fear of being left alone, fear of giving a talk, fear of children leaving home. What is important is working through the fear and facing reality. Natural quartz adjusts its vibrational level to the person using it, so it can help you see through your fears, and achieve what you want.

Crystal healing

To release a current fear, sit cross-legged in a darkened room and hold your crystal in your hands; feel it aligning with your energies. Look deeply into your stone: staring into clear quartz is believed to enhance your psychic abilities. Now place it on your fear center—the solar plexus in your upper abdomen—and see your current fear. Let your doubts about this challenge flit through your mind. Now ask your stone to give you ways to handle it. Feel the pleasing emotions as your crystal shows you positive solutions. Cleanse the crystal well after the session (see pages 149–153).

ALTERNATIVE FEAR-RELEASING CRYSTALS TO USE

Moss agate: releases fear and encourages personal growth

Apophyllite: dissolves negative thought patterns and worries

Chiastolite: calms fear, helps with facing reality

Balancing your emotions with sodalite

Sodalite is a dark blue stone, flecked with pieces of white calcite. It can be confused with the mystical lapis lazuli crystal as it also contains pyrite, but it doesn't have the gold specks that lapis often has. A stone of the mind, sodalite dispels mental clutter and promotes rational thoughts. It is a supreme balancer of the emotions, helping to bring them back under control when we lose good communication with our inner selves. Noticeable signs are becoming irrationally angry because of not dealing with a past upset or crying because of a suppressed hurt.

Crystal healing

Sodalite brings issues from your past to the surface and releases them, repairing your fragile emotions. Sit in a quiet room and take your sodalite crystal in your hands and hold it to your chest for about 5–10 minutes. Close your eyes and connect with your inner child who is about five and who holds all your shame and guilt. Ask them what past incident is causing your emotional upsets. As they tell you, focus on the event and let your crystal send blue healing energy out to release the pain and transform it into love and self-acceptance. Feel a wonderful emotional peace come over you as you slowly come back into the room. Cleanse your crystal of any negativity (see pages 149–153).

CRYSTAL FACTS

CRYSTAL TO USE: sodalite (dark blue, blue/white) variegated stone

AVAILABILITY: commonly available

QUALITIES OF STONE: disperses fear, calms the mind, enhances self-expression, increases rational thoughts, promotes courage, clears old mental patterns, soothes panic attacks, balances emotions, encourages self-acceptance

Rough

HEALTH BENEFITS: aids functioning of the pancreas, balances endocrine system and metabolism, detoxifies the lymphatic system, lowers blood pressure, treats throat and digestive problems

WHERE TO PLACE THE CRYSTAL: on the heart in the middle of the chest

ALTERNATIVE EMOTIONAL-BALANCING CRYSTALS TO USE

Chrysocolla: works on guilt and brings in joy

Citrine: releases negative traits, overcomes anger

Rhodonite: creates emotional balance and promotes love

Asking forgiveness with rhodochrosite

Polished

Rhodochrosite is a wonderful crystal for bringing repressed upsets to the surface, healing emotional scars and allowing you to move on positively. Interestingly, its alternative name, Inca Rose, may have derived from its formation in ancient Inca silver mines, where the rose-colored crystal grew as stalactites and stalagmites. Like rhodochrosite, our secrets and worries may be hidden deep within our consciousness. Holding past resentments can literally eat away at your body, and in time if they are not released, may cause physical illness. You need to forgive ex-lovers for letting you down, past friends for not supporting you enough, parents for being overcritical and yourself for not achieving everything you wanted. Sometimes we do not want to forgive, but trying starts the healing process and allows us to live more fully in the present.

CRYSTAL FACTS

CRYSTAL TO USE: rhodochrosite (pink/orange), banded structure, can be tumbled, polished

AVAILABILITY: commonly available

QUALITIES OF STONE: encourages change, heals emotional wounds, releases hidden feelings, inspires forgiveness, brings in love

HEALTH BENEFITS: helps asthmatic and respiratory problems, improves eyesight, stabilizes blood pressure, relieves migraines

WHERE TO PLACE THE CRYSTAL: on your heart

Crystal healing

Work on deep-held resentments one at a time or you may find it overwhelming. Lie down, close your eyes, and hold the crystal to your heart. Visualize a darkened stage and put the person you want to forgive on it. Now see good things happening to him or her, and send the healing vibrations from your crystal to them. Feel the resentment lifting from your heart and being replaced with love. See this person laughing before they fade from the stage.

ALTERNATIVE FORGIVENESS CRYSTALS TO USE

Pink calcite: a forgiving stone that releases sadness

Chrysoprase: aids compassion and acceptance of others

Celestite: resolves conflict, bringing inner peace

Removing old belief patterns with green calcite

Green calcite has many different uses. It can balance the male and female polarities and ground the emotions. Many spiritualists say it improves astral projection when your soul goes traveling at night.

Belief patterns can be imposed on us in childhood from parental influence. Some are positive but many adversely affect our adult lives. Green calcite is a special healing crystal that dissolves fixed beliefs and deep inner programming. The stone's gentle green emissions can dissolve the rigidity of an old belief pattern to allow a more fulfilling one to come in. For example, a workaholic lifestyle created from a childhood criticism, "You need to achieve more," can be transformed into a career with an enjoyable work/life balance by recognizing and letting go of this unwanted belief. Green calcite gives you the strength to recognize things that no longer serve you.

Crystal cure

To do a belief-releasing ceremony, sit in a quiet room and burn two green candles. Pick up your calcite stone, hold it to your heart, feeling its balancing, calming vibrations, and gaze into the flames. Think of the belief pattern that is adversely affecting your life and sense your crystal's purifying properties helping to melt it in the flames. Now see a positive belief appearing in the flames such as, "I am successful in everything I do." Slowly come to, remembering to cleanse your crystal to keep it positive (see pages 149–153).

Rough

CRYSTAL FACTS

CRYSTAL TO USE: green calcite, translucent, waxy feel, often with bands, sometimes treated with acid to improve color, can be tumbled

AVAILABILITY: commonly available

QUALITIES OF STONE: balances the emotions, takes away fear, reduces stress, soothes anxiety, aids intuition, removes rigid beliefs and old programming, increases psychic abilities, stimulates memory

HEALTH BENEFITS: releases body toxins, boosts kidneys, spleen, and pancreas, helps arthritis and ligament problems, calms fever, soothes burns and inflammations

WHERE TO PLACE THE CRYSTAL: on your Heart chakra in the middle of your chest

ALTERNATIVE RELEASING CRYSTALS TO USE

Pietersite: removes beliefs and conditioning set by other people

Sodalite: releases old mental patterns and creates new insights

Smoky quartz: releases beliefs from the psyche that no longer serve you

Revitalizing your energy with kyanite

Rough

CRYSTAL FACTS

CRYSTAL TO USE: blue or green kyanite, transparent or opaque, striated

AVAILABILITY: blue kyanite commonly available; green kyanite can be hard to find

QUALITIES OF STONE: promotes mental clarity, calms emotions, balances chakras and clears blockages, helps meditation, dispels anger, restores energy, stimulates spiritual energy and intuition

HEALTH BENEFITS: relieves pain, calms fevers, treats muscular pain, stimulates endocrine system, lowers blood pressure

WHERE TO PLACE THE CRYSTAL: on your Heart chakra (middle of chest) and Third eye chakra (middle of forehead)

Kyanite is a courageous crystal that can help you to find your soul's purpose. The stone is thought to work with archangel Michael and his sword of truth, which cuts away unwanted mental or spiritual attitudes, and is a more powerful sword than King Arthur's sword Excalibur. A calming, compassionate crystal, kyanite also amplifies and transmits energy, helping to clear any emotional blockages from your energetic meridians or pathways and balancing your main energy centers, your chakras. If you are suffering from a lack of vitality after a demanding time at work meeting pressured deadlines, or are taking time out from an upsetting relationship, this stone can boost your energy field and bring its flow back into balance.

Crystal healing

To revitalize your energy, lie in a darkened room and pick up your crystal and feel its vibrating emissions. Hold it to your Heart chakra for 5–10 minutes, feeling the stone clearing any emotional confusion or trauma and increasing your energy levels. Now move it to the Third eye chakra for a further 5 minutes to release any worries or anger here and to stimulate mental clarity and positive brain energy to deal effectively with your life once more. Some healers have found that kyanite does not retain negativity, so it never needs cleansing.

ALTERNATIVE ENERGY-BOOSTING CRYSTALS TO USE

Garnet: energizes, cleanses, and balances the chakras

Fire opal: reenergizes, bringing change and progress

Natural quartz: regulates and amplifies energy flow, dissolves blockages

Protecting your aura with apache tear obsidian

Polished

CRYSTAL FACTS

CRYSTAL TO USE: apache tear obsidian (black), translucent, often water-worn

AVAILABILITY: commonly available

QUALITIES OF STONE: absorbs and disperses negative energy, promotes inner growth, reduces stress, blocks geopathic stress, releases mental pain, relieves sadness and loneliness, helps to face dark side, strengthens aura

HEALTH BENEFITS: aids functioning of the stomach and intestines, reduces muscles spasms, detoxes the body, relieves arthritis, joint problems and muscle cramps

WHERE TO PLACE THE CRYSTAL: move the crystal round your aura

Made from volcanic glass, apache tear obsidian is a "truthful" crystal that shows your strengths and weaknesses. Many people are drawn to obsidian because it protects the aura—our subtle energetic field. The aura is a "buffer" for our bodies (see also page 65). It has several layers and changes colors to reflect our fluctutating moods: the brighter our aura's colors, the healthier we are.

Crystal healing

To shield your aura, stand by your bed in the morning holding your crystal, and feel its supportive energies. Ask the stone to create an impenetrable barrier around you, then move it all around your aura, from your head, out to the right side and down to your feet, then all around your left. Now visualize a powerful white light coming from your Crown chakra filling your body with a spiritual energy that lasts all day. Cleanse your crystal well after use (see pages 149–153).

ALTERNATIVE AURA-PROTECTING CRYSTALS TO USE

Aquamarine: balances chakras, shields the aura

Hematite: deflects negative energies from the aura

Kunzite: banishes unwanted energies from the aura

Clearing meditation with sunstone

Polished

CRYSTAL FACTS

CRYSTAL TO USE: sunstone, (yellow, orange, red/ brown), transparent, clear, or opaque, can be small and tumbled

AVAILABILITY: sunstone from Oregon is commonly available from specialist stores

QUALITIES OF STONE: joyful stone, restores the spirit, clears the chakras, brings luck and good fortune, removes attachments, gives self-empowerment, an antidepressant, lifts black moods, promotes enthusiasm

HEALTH BENEFITS: good for heart and blood circulation, aids aching bones or joints, can increase sexual energy, helps organs, helps sore throats

WHERE TO PLACE THE CRYSTAL: hold in hands in lap

A warm, joyful crystal, nowadays sunstone (a lemony, transparent stone) mainly comes from Oregon and India, where it is a golden stone, similar to moonstone. You can only feel good around this crystal. In the past it was prized as a lucky stone that attracted the influences of benevolent gods. We all have emotional hang-ups that drain our energy, and sunstone is a crystal that removes psychic attachments from our aura (energy field), sending them back with love to past partners or overbearing parents. This sunny stone can cleanse you at the end the day when you are emotionally and mentally exhausted from work stress or maybe the pain of ending a close friendship.

Crystal healing

To clear your mind each evening, sit cross-legged in a darkened living room. Burn some relaxing lavender essential oil and light a candle. Hold your crystal in your lap, and take some slow, deep breaths from your diaphragm. Look deeply at your stone, then close your 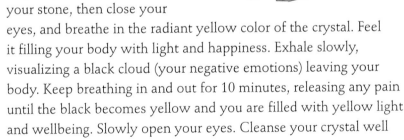 eyes, and breathe in the radiant yellow color of the crystal. Feel it filling your body with light and happiness. Exhale slowly, visualizing a black cloud (your negative emotions) leaving your body. Keep breathing in and out for 10 minutes, releasing any pain until the black becomes yellow and you are filled with yellow light and wellbeing. Slowly open your eyes. Cleanse your crystal well (see pages 149–153).

ALTERNATIVE CLEARING CRYSTALS TO USE

Amber: powerful cleanser, brings wisdom

Agate: clears negativity and bitterness (right: brown agate)

Fluorite: purifies and removes stress (right: green fluorite)

Letting go of sorrows with onyx

The name onyx comes from the Greek *onux*, meaning fingernail or claw. In Roman legend, Venus, the goddess of love, was sleeping and her son, Cupid, cut her fingernails, leaving the clippings on the ground. As no heavenly entity can die, the gods transformed the clippings into the stone we know as onyx. It is a balancing crystal that gives strength to the user suffering extreme emotional stress. A releaser of pain, it gets rid of past hurts that eat away inside you, stopping you from enjoying your current life and being fully in the moment. We all need to mourn but constantly reliving an upsetting childhood or an old love affair is only holding you back. Black onyx is a supportive stone that pushes you to take that step forward and express these hurts.

Polished egg

Crystal healing

To liberate past hurts, sit in a quiet room and pick up your black onyx crystal. Turn the stone over in your hands feeling its wise vibrations. Close your eyes and focus on your first hurt, feel the emotions, see that person or situation, be back in that moment. Now ask the stone for its help in releasing this trauma, to heal your hurt and to learn a lesson from it. Let the images fade and with them all your pain. Work on further hurts, or slowly come to. Cleanse your crystal well after use (see pages 149–153).

CRYSTAL FACTS

CRYSTAL TO USE: green onyx, banded, often polished

AVAILABILITY: commonly available

QUALITIES OF STONE: eliminates grief, encourages self-control, promotes happiness and abundance, relieves stress, helps you to become master of your own destiny, releases past trauma, encourages fidelity

HEALTH BENEFITS: aids hearing problems, benefits the heart, heals ulcers, strengthens teeth and bones, works on blood disorders

WHERE TO PLACE THE CRYSTAL: hold in hands in lap

ALTERNATIVE PAIN-RELEASING CRYSTALS TO USE

Pink tourmaline:
relieves emotional pain, cleanses destructive emotions

Chrysocolla:
heals heartache, releases repressed emotions

Promoting self-love with pink tourmaline

Rough

Tourmalines are precious crystals that often display beautiful color. According to an ancient Egyptian legend, tourmaline traveled along a rainbow, collecting its delightful mix of colors on its way from the earth's crust to the sun. Holding up a tourmaline to the light, it is unusually transparent from the side but opaque from either end. Pink tourmaline is a wise and inspiring crystal that attracts love and friendship. You may find it easy to love other people but tend to hang onto all the criticisms received from your parents and friends and see yourself as imperfect or unworthy. This crystal teaches you that you need to love yourself before others will truly love you.

CRYSTAL FACTS

CRYSTAL TO USE: pink tourmaline, transparent or opaque, often striated and hexagonal

AVAILABILITY: commonly available from specialist stores

QUALITIES OF STONE: very protective stone, inspires and aids concentration, balances the chakras, promotes self-confidence, gives understanding of emotions, promotes self-love, brings peace and relaxation

HEALTH BENEFITS: harmonizes endocrine system, encourages sleep, aids the lymphatic and digestive systems, treats the heart and lungs, improves skin

WHERE TO PLACE THE CRYSTAL: on your Heart chakra in the middle of your chest

Crystal healing

To love yourself, you need to reprogram the self-criticism that stems from your subconscious so that you can give and receive love freely. The pink tourmaline crystal links to Venus, the goddess of love, and it is hard not to love yourself when holding this tender stone. To work on loving yourself more, stand in front of a large mirror. Hold the crystal to your heart and say 20 times looking directly into the mirror, "I love you as you are." Feel the compassionate pink vibrations from your stone melting any destructive feelings held in your subconscious and opening your heart to love. Practice the affirmation daily until you really believe what you are saying. Always cleanse your crystal after use to remove any negative emotions (see pages 149–153).

ALTERNATIVE SELF-LOVE CRYSTALS TO USE

Rose quartz: facilitates deep inner healing and self-love

Rhodonite: transmutes self-criticism into self-love

Magnesite: opens Heart chakra and encourages self-love

Letting go of guilt with peridot

A delicate, transparent stone in varying shades of yellow-green, red and brown, peridot has legendary curative powers. As far back as Roman times, medicine drunk from goblets decorated with this crystal were believed to increase in potency. A wonderful cleanser, peridot clears the mind and lets you release things from your past. So if you have hidden guilt lingering in your subconscious, it can be affecting your adult life. You may have stolen money as a child from your mother, and now money slips through your fingers, or you may have been unkind to a child at school and now find it hard to get on with your work colleagues. This crystal clears away guilt and teaches you that hanging on to old emotion is counterproductive.

Rough

CRYSTAL FACTS

CRYSTAL TO USE: peridot, also known as chrysolite, olivine (olive green, yellow/green, red, brown, deep yellow)

AVAILABILITY: commonly available, but good crystals are hard to find

QUALITIES OF STONE: increases intuition, stimulates the mind, reduces stress and negativity, clears hurts, cleanses guilt, increases confidence and assertive behavior

HEALTH BENEFITS: increases tissue regeneration, aids the heart, pancreas, spleen, liver, and adrenals, boosts metabolism, helps digestion, improves skin texture

WHERE TO PLACE THE CRYSTAL: hold in hands

Crystal healing

To heal your inner guilt, sit in a quiet room and pick up your peridot crystal and study its wonderful green color that can heal your emotions and bring gentle regrowth. Close your eyes and see yourself in a peaceful field. Sit on the grass and ask your sub-conscious to join you. Ask it to show you the guilt that still affects you, then allow these images or feelings to flow through you. Now ask your crystal to release cleansing vibrations to remove this guilt, and let you admit the mistake and move on. Send love to your subconscious, and sense a deep warm glow, then slowly come back into the room. Always cleanse your crystal well (see pages 149–153).

Rough

ALTERNATIVE GUILT-RELEASING CRYSTALS TO USE

Chrysocolla: a sustaining stone that liberates inner guilt

Sodalite: transforms, and lets go of core fears and guilt

Chiastolite: clears hidden guilt, balances emotions

Increasing self-esteem with moss agate

Moss agate is believed to feed the soul. Known as the gardener's stone, this clear crystal has a deep connection with nature because of its curious plantlike markings. A prime ingredient in magic spells to promote happiness and a long life, it is a wonderful crystal to balance the emotions and bring new beginnings. A weight problem can ruin your self-image, and constant criticism from your parents can drain self-esteem. This stone works on dispelling your inner fears and feelings of inadequacy.

Rough

Crystal healing

Moss agate is a crystal of self-realization; it releases fear, making you appreciate your true worth and see your inner radiance. To work on improving your self-worth, sit in a quiet room, pick up your crystal, and hold it to your Solar plexus chakra: the place where we take all the emotional blows in life. Hold it there for about 10 minutes, feeling this stabilizing crystal boosting your positive characteristics and dispelling any depression. Use your crystal every day for a week until you feel you can take on the world once more. After healing, always cleanse your stone well to keep its energy bright (see pages 149–153).

CRYSTAL FACTS

CRYSTAL TO USE: moss agate (green, blue, red, yellow, brown), transparent or translucent, has foliage or mosslike pattern, can be tumbled

AVAILABILITY: commonly available

QUALITIES OF STONE: attracts money and abundance, increases strength and courage, inspires the soul, improves ego and self-esteem, brings emotional balance, reduces negativity

HEALTH BENEFITS: relieves exhaustion, helps neck and back problems, cleanses the blood, strengthens the immune system, reduces fever, treats colds and flu

WHERE TO PLACE THE CRYSTAL: on your Solar plexus chakra in your upper abdomen

Polished

ALTERNATIVE SELF-ESTEEM CRYSTALS TO USE

Citrine: reduces sensitivity to criticism, raises self-esteem

Rhodochrosite: alleviates painful feelings, improves self-worth

Boosting confidence with chrysocolla

Chrysocolla, a stone of peace and wisdom, removes negative emotions—in chakra healing, using chrysocolla on the Third eye chakra (between the brows) helps promote inner knowledge and psychic vision.

You can use this bright stone to correct any sub-conscious imbalances or destructive programming you may be harboring. We are all very good at criticizing ourselves, but often we do not praise our good points. Our self-image can be poor and we may find it hard to be positive about our bodies. Often this negative patterning, or lack of confidence, is what we felt about ourselves as young children, perhaps unconsciously instilled by parents and contemporaries.

Rough

Crystal healing

Working with a chrysocolla can help to change your self-image and increase self-esteem. Take hold of your crystal and turn it over a few times in your hands to feel its energy. Lie down, close your eyes, and place the stone on your Throat chakra (see also page 62) in the middle of your throat near your jaw for about 5 minutes. Focus on letting go of what has caused your bad self-image, and visualize yourself as a happy, positive person. Feel the vibrations of the crystal working with you, releasing your old pattern, increasing your personal power and confidence. Repeat daily for a week until you feel you can take on the world.

CRYSTAL FACTS

CRYSTAL TO USE: chrysocolla (green, blue, turquoise), opaque, often with bands, generally polished or tumbled

AVAILABILITY: commonly available

QUALITIES OF STONE: takes away fears or guilt, brings balance, releases nervous tension, increases self awareness, and brings confidence

HEALTH BENEFITS: soothes digestive problems and arthritic conditions, reduces period pains and premenstrual tension, heals infections, calms burns

WHERE TO PLACE THE CRYSTAL: on your throat

ALTERNATIVE CONFIDENCE-BUILDING CRYSTALS TO USE

Agate: brings self-acceptance and builds confidence (right: brown agate)

Garnet: dissolves old behavioral patterns, increases self-confidence

Tiger's eye: heals issues of self-worth and helps recognition of abilities

Visualizing a positive future with labradorite

Labradorite is a mystical crystal that is named after Labrador, a Canadian town, which mines the stone. A plain grayish color, it shows glorious flashes of colors such as blue and yellow when held to the light. A transformational stone, labradorite works on your Third eye chakra: your intuitive center increasing your psychic abilities. It is a crystal that attracts success for its owner, so if you have what seems like an impossible dream, perhaps owning a villa abroad, becoming an artist, or training as a ski instructor, working with labradorite can make this dream a reality.

CRYSTAL FACTS

CRYSTAL TO USE: labradorite (grayish with flashes of blue/yellow), also known as spectrolite (white with blue/yellow flashes), transparent, can be small and tumbled

AVAILABILITY: commonly available

Polished egg

QUALITIES OF STONE: unblocks chakras, induces peaceful sleep, increases intuition and psychic vision, promotes courage, perception, and visualization techniques, dispels insecurities, inspires imagination

HEALTH BENEFITS: balances hormones, alleviates menstrual pain, reduces blood pressure, controls metabolism, treats colds and eye problems

WHERE TO PLACE THE CRYSTAL: hold in hands

Rough

Crystal energizing

Living your dream as though it were already happening can give out the positive energies to attract what you want. Visualizing your dream also fixes it firmly in your subconscious, endorsing what you want. Labradorite increases your spiritual connection, strengthening your visualization techniques to bring in your desired change. Sit in a quiet room and close your eyes. Pick up your stone, feeling its wisdom and strength. Breathe deeply and visualize your dream: see yourself having a drink on the terrace in your villa in the sun, or leading a party of skiers down the mountain. Let your stone increase your imagination, helping you to be there, feeling and absorbing the sensations. Step out of the scene and observe it from the outside, then step back until you are really part of it. Slowly step out of the scene and come back into the room. Practice regularly with your crystal until your dream comes true.

ALTERNATIVE VISUALIZATION CRYSTALS TO USE

Magnesite: place on Third eye chakra on forehead for increased imagery

Ruby: helps follow dreams, stimulates pineal gland for visualization

Amethyst: has a high spiritual vibration, enhances visualization

Calming fears when flying with rhodochrosite

The pretty pink banded colors of rhodochrosite are caused by the element manganese that blends with the stone. One way the crystal is formed is when manganese is dissolved by groundwater and combines with a carbonate material that drops off the ceilings and crevices underground forming stalagmites and stalactites. Known as another powerful love stone, rhodochrosite also alleviates emotional upset or stress, and can help to ease a fear of flying. Even though statistically it is a far safer mode of transport than driving a car, it is often the lack of control, or having to put their trust in a pilot, that can make people anxious and upset when they step on a plane.

Polished

CRYSTAL FACTS

CRYSTAL TO USE: rhodochrosite (pink), banded, can be tumbled

QUALITIES OF STONE: heals emotional upsets or stress, encourages forgiveness, attracts love, helps to face reality and confront irrational fears, eases loneliness and heartache

HEALTH BENEFITS: improves eyesight, helps functioning of kidneys, pancreas, spleen, and sexual organs, aids blood detoxification, improves asthma and respiratory disease, improves skin, relieves migraine, balances thyroid

WHERE TO PLACE THE CRYSTAL: hold in hands

Crystal healing

To cope with any anxieties about flying, such as during turbulence or going over water, take out your rhodochrosite crystal as soon as you sit down on the plane. This gentle, loving pink stone has the power to release your irrational fears, leaving you calm and centered. As the plane takes off, hold your crystal tightly and concentrate on releasing any muscular tension in your body with your stone's help. Start at your feet, breathe in deeply, and as you breathe out visualize any tightness flowing out of them. Move on to your calves, then your thighs, breathing in and relaxing any taut muscles as you breathe out. Work through your body until you reach your head. Sense your crystal's compassionate vibrations working with you, soothing mind and body and releasing your emotional upset. Leave it on your lap for the flight, holding it tightly whenever you feel distressed. Cleanse the stone after use to keep it working well (see pages 149–153).

ALTERNATIVE FEAR-REDUCING CRYSTALS TO USE

Orange calcite: alleviates stress, takes away fear

Amazonite: calms nervous system, takes away worries

Onyx: calms mental stress, reduces overpowering fears

Dealing with jet lag with snow quartz

Quartz is the supreme healing crystal. In early Britain they were often called "star stones" and were a part of folk magic rituals. The stones were collected with some water from a stream and boiled together. The cooled water was drunk as an elixir to keep illness at bay.

Snow quartz has a more gentle vibration than clear quartz, but still works on regulating your body energy. A crystal that balances your body, it brings your biorhythms (your body's natural rhythms) back to normal after you have crossed different time zones when traveling long-haul. The symptoms of jet lag are debilitating, often disturbing your sleep patterns, making you feel tired or physically and mentally low.

Rough

Crystal cure

To restore your body's natural rhythms after crossing time zones, take hold of your snow quartz crystal and request its help to regain your normal energy levels. Place the stone under your pillow at night so that its slow vibrations can harmonize your body's rhythms throughout the night. If you still suffer during the day, carry your crystal around with you. Cleanse well after use (see pages 149–153).

CRYSTAL FACTS

CRYSTAL TO USE: snow quartz (white), known as milky quartz and quartzite; can be crystalline form or pebble

AVAILABILITY: commonly available

QUALITIES OF STONE: balances emotions, clears negativity from aura, gently energizes

HEALTH BENEFITS: aids functioning of the organs and recuperation from illness, stimulates immune system, soothes burns

WHERE TO PLACE THE CRYSTAL: under your pillow, in your pocket or handbag

Polished heart

ALTERNATIVE JET-LAG CRYSTALS TO USE

Black tourmaline: releases toxins, reduces effects of jet lag

Amethyst: soothes nervous system, boosts memory, and aids sleeping

Coping with daily travel stress with brown jasper

Jasper is a form of chalcedony (part of the quartz family). When you look carefully at this pretty stone, it has beautiful color variations. In the past, its light and dark brown markings meant that this stone was often referred to as Egyptian marble.

A wonderful nurturing and protective crystal, jasper absorbs any negative energy and clears any environmental pollution that surrounds you. Traveling by car, train, or bus to work, meetings, or while doing the school run can be very demanding, and feelings of frustration at delays or traffic jams can build up inside you as your stress levels soar. Carrying a brown jasper crystal with you sustains and supports you during your daily onslaught with travel, slowing your nervous system and controlling your anger. This supportive quality was well known in the past when the stone was carried to drive away evil spirits and protect against venomous snake or spider bites. Jasper also brings you good luck if you wear it in the shape of an arrowhead.

Crystal cure

Your brown jasper crystal will help you get to grips with any situation that you encounter on your journey. When a problem arises, or if you start to get upset at another delay, take out and hold your stone for a few minutes until you feel your stress abating and you start to become more relaxed.

CRYSTAL FACTS

CRYSTAL TO USE: brown jasper, opaque, patterned, can be tumbled

AVAILABILITY: commonly available

QUALITIES OF STONE: absorbs negative energy, clears environmental pollution, protects and grounds energies

HEALTH BENEFITS: boosts immune system, aids circulatory and digestive systems

WHERE TO PLACE THE CRYSTAL: your pocket, purse, or workbag

ALTERNATIVE TRAVEL-STRESS CRYSTALS TO USE

Blue lace agate: dissolves mental stress, calms nervous system

Golden topaz: releases all tension and stabilizes the emotions

Celestite: calms the mind and gets rid of any worries

Harmonizing your car with amber

Hippocrates, the ancient Greek father of medicine, wrote in the 5th century BCE about the healing powers of amber, and native shamans in many cultures have used its protective qualities in rituals for years. Sometimes called the honey stone because it is so soft and warm to touch, amber generates a flowing, calming energy and is said to contain the heat and power of many suns, absorbing negativity and protecting the user from harm. It generates courage, self-confidence, and a joy of life, so placing this harmonizing crystal in your car can help maintain a supportive atmosphere, as you drive around for work or transport fractious children to school.

Crystal healing

To use in the car, first have a clear-out as the crystal will find it hard to battle against stagnant energies. Now take hold of your amber crystal, feel its loving and generous power filling your body, and ask it to become your protective talisman when driving. Place it on the dashboard or in a pocket, letting its uplifting energies form a gold ring around your car. Cleanse it every few months to keep it working at full strength (see pages 149–153).

Polished

CRYSTAL FACTS

CRYSTAL TO USE: amber (yellow, orange, golden/brown), transparent or opaque; some have insects or vegetation trapped inside, as it is actually a fossilized tree resin

AVAILABILITY: commonly available but expensive; beware of manmade copies (see page 85)

QUALITIES OF STONE: promotes compassion, relieves depression, cleanses the environment, transmutes negative into positive energies, stimulates a positive mental state

HEALTH BENEFITS: boosts the endocrine system, soothes earache and rheumatism, eases stomach problems, treats the kidneys, spleen, and bladder, has antibiotic properties as an essence

WHERE TO PLACE THE CRYSTAL: on the dashboard or in a side pocket

ALTERNATIVE PROTECTIVE CRYSTALS TO USE

Fire agate: grounding stone that creates a secure and safe ambience

Amethyst: absorbs negative energies, calms and protects

Jasper: nurturing stone, grounds energies, provides protection (right: red jasper)

Promoting calm when driving with blue lace agate

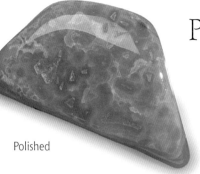

Polished

CRYSTAL FACTS

CRYSTAL TO USE: blue lace agate, banded, can be small and tumbled

AVAILABILITY: commonly available

QUALITIES OF STONE: improves vitality, increases ego and self-esteem, restores calm and peace and relieves stress, encourages open expression of feelings, strengthens mind

HEALTH BENEFITS: reduces infections, inflammation, and fever, heals thyroid, throat, and lymph disturbances, treats arthritis and joint problems, stimulates digestion, prevents gastritis

WHERE TO PLACE THE CRYSTAL: on the dashboard or in your pocket

The beautiful pale blue lace agate with its attractive striped patterns was worn in ancient times as a truth amulet to make sure that the only words you spoke were pure. Renowned as a peace-bringer, it links to the soothing element of water, so using the stone can help you relax and de-stress. In today's busy world this crystal's calming influence can defuse any fiery emotions that arise from traffic incidents when you are driving. Sitting in endless traffic jams, or experiencing road rage from another driver can make you stressed and angry. Anger can make you drive less carefully, but carrying a blue agate crystal, or leaving one in the car, can reduce tension and ensure you keep your emotions under control.

Crystal healing

Place your stone on the dashboard of your car or leave in your pocket. If you get angry because of a driving upset, stop the car safely, then start to gaze into the soothing depths of your blue agate crystal. Take some deep breaths and feel how this supportive stone is lowering your blood pressure, and neutralizing your irritation and anger so that you can continue driving calmly once more. If you are getting exasperated in a long traffic line, turn the stone over in your hand like a worry bead to lessen your anxieties or frustrations. Cleanse the crystal regularly after prolonged use (see pages 149–153).

ALTERNATIVE CALMING CRYSTALS TO USE

Aquamarine: quiets the mind, reduces stress, invokes tolerance

Howlite: teaches patience, cools rage and anger

Blue tiger's eye: calms mind and takes away stress

Keeping safe with jet

Polished

Jet has long been known for its protective qualities and its ability to absorb bad vibrations. In fact, in ancient times, wives of fishermen kept a jet amulet at home so that their husbands would return safe from the sea. The protective amulet of travelers, it is thought to look after you when you are out alone at night. So in today's world it can be a reassuring talisman to have with you when you are traveling on public transport late at night or if you need to walk or cycle in less populated areas on your own where you can feel a bit unsafe.

CRYSTAL FACTS

CRYSTAL TO USE: jet (black), normally small and polished, made from fossilized wood

AVAILABILITY: commonly available

QUALITIES OF STONE: reduces fears, prevents depressive tendencies, helps to grieve, protects from violence, can guard against bad dreams, looks after travelers, assists spiritual development

HEALTH BENEFITS: reduces swellings in legs and feet, relieves neuralgia and toothache, treats colds and migraines, reduces menstrual problems, alleviates stomach troubles

WHERE TO PLACE THE CRYSTAL: carry in bag or pocket or wear it as jewelry

Crystal healing

A black, glasslike stone, jet is actually made from fossilized wood. When worn continuously as jewelry it is said to absorb part of the person's soul, so if you inherit or buy some old jet, always cleanse it well before wearing.

To protect you when traveling, keep your stone in your bag or pocket or wear it as jewelry. Each time before you go out, hold the crystal in your hands and tune into its caring vibrations. Ask it to create a white protective shield around you to repel attackers, keeping you safe from violence at all times. If you suffer from nightmares, keep a jet stone beside your bed at night to soothe your troubled emotions. Always cleanse the crystal regularly to keep it vibrant (see pages 149–153).

ALTERNATIVE PROTECTIVE CRYSTALS TO USE

Fire opal: strengthens personal power, protects from danger

Garnet: a protective amulet, can warn of approaching dangers

Bloodstone: protective stone that shows how to avoid dangerous situations

Energizing a hotel room with natural quartz

Many past civilizations, such as the ancient Christians, revered the healing power of quartz, making their relics from the crystal, which they believed to be fossilized ice. Natural quartz is such a versatile crystal. It is the main crystal of crystal healing and has the ability to take in any low-energy vibrations and transmute and amplify them to a higher level to which you will react favorably. It can also disperse any negativity in the environment, making it a great crystal to use if you travel regularly and stay in different hotel rooms that can still have the energetic "imprints" of all the people who have stayed in them. These can leave an anonymous feel or possibly a sad, lingering unhappiness about the space that needs to be cleared.

Cluster

CRYSTAL FACTS

CRYSTAL TO USE: natural quartz (clear or milky), pointed, may be striated crystals or clusters

AVAILABILITY: commonly available

QUALITIES OF STONE: disperses negativity in the environment, receives, transmits, and amplifies energy, aids meditation, boosts intuition, protects against electromagnetic stress, stimulates concentration, increases psychic abilities

HEALTH BENEFITS: powerful general healer, boosts the immune system, can relieve toothache and reduce a temperature, soothes the pain of burns

WHERE TO PLACE THE CRYSTAL: on your nightstand or bedside cabinet

Crystal healing

When you check into a hotel room, open all the windows to let the air do a basic cleansing. Hold your natural quartz crystal in your hands and ask it to use its powers to "spring clean" the room, removing

Polished

any traces of the previous occupant and lifting its energies. Place the stone by your bed, or if the weather is sunny, leave it briefly on a windowsill and let it amplify the glorious rays of the sun. Leave the room for an hour or so and then come back in, noticing how vibrant and inviting the atmosphere has become. Cleanse the stone after use (see pages 149–153).

ALTERNATIVE ENERGIZING CRYSTALS TO USE

Amethyst: blocks negative environmental energies, energizes with love

Green fluorite: absorbs negative energies, creates harmony

Malachite: takes in negative vibrations, transmutes them to radiate positivity

Boosting vitality when walking with orange calcite

The word calcite comes from the Latin word *calx* and the Greek word *chalix*, which mean lime. The calcite crystal is commonly found embedded in limestone and marble. Orange calcite is a bright, stimulating crystal that can boost your creativity and bring emotional balance. It is associated with the sun, and its warm, orange color, at the hot end of the color spectrum, is a potent energizer. For walking it is the perfect stone to take with you as it can give an instant energy burst to your muscles when your legs start to ache or feel tired.

Rough

Crystal energizing

If your legs are tiring on a long walk, take some time out to have a brief rest and recharge your batteries. Do a few stretches and massage your calves. Take out your orange calcite crystal and hold it in your hands until you feel a slight tingling or pulsating—this is how it starts to energize you. Now hold the crystal to each leg for a few minutes to ease the muscle tension and increase the blood flow, so that you can walk on with renewed vigor. If you regularly suffer muscle tiredness when walking, tape a crystal to each leg as you walk to ease the pain.

CRYSTAL FACTS

CRYSTAL TO USE: orange calcite, translucent, waxy appearance, occasionally tumbled

AVAILABILITY: commonly available

QUALITIES OF STONE: cleanses and energizes, combats lethargy, encourages action, relieves fear, aids depression

HEALTH BENEFITS: aids the kidneys and bladder, heals reproductive and digestive disorders, alleviates irritable bowel syndrome, aids fatigue, increases energy

WHERE TO PLACE THE CRYSTAL: in your pocket

ALTERNATIVE REVITALIZING CRYSTALS TO USE

Ruby: restores energy when exhausted, boosts a healthy blood circulation

Kyanite: restores physical energy and activates organs

Reducing cell phone emissions with amazonite

Polished

Amazonite, or Amazon stone, is known to protect against cellphone emissions because of its amazing filtering ability. Cellphones emit electromagnetic radiation to which our brains, in particular, are sensitive. Research has yet to prove whether these emissions can be harmful, but people who use their cellphones for long periods have reported symptoms of fatigue, headaches, and burning sensations in the area where the phone was held.

The energy of amazonite can help dissipate cellphone emissions, along with calming the brain and nervous system; it is also reputed to help repair the body and heal the aura. In magical ritual, amazonite is associated with success—so this crystal may just bring a little more sparkle to all your phone conversations.

CRYSTAL FACTS

CRYSTAL TO USE: amazonite, has veins, sometimes tumbled

AVAILABILITY: commonly available

QUALITIES OF STONE: powerful filter, absorbs cellphone radiation

HEALTH BENEFITS: aids osteoporosis, helps tooth decay, eases muscular spasms

WHERE TO PLACE THE CRYSTAL: taped to your cellphone

Crystal cure

Use a cellphone only when really necessary, and try to buy a phone that has one of the lowest recorded emissions of radiation. Use a hands-free device and make shorter calls when possible to minimize potential harm. To reduce health risks further, tape a small amazonite crystal to your phone—the least conspicuous area is on the back of the phone. Amazonite will work hard for you to absorb and neutralize some of the radiation that a cellphone emits when it is held to your ear.

ALTERNATIVE RADIATION-REDUCING CRYSTALS TO USE

Aventurine: defuses negativity, reduces cell phone emissions

Kunzite: provides a protective shield, blocks radiation from cell phones

Black tourmaline: disperses stress, ameliorates cell phone emissions

Reducing Arian recklessness with purple fluorite

Polished

CRYSTAL FACTS

CRYSTAL TO USE: purple fluorite, transparent, cubic, or octahedral

AVAILABILITY: commonly available

QUALITIES OF STONE: effectively grounds and balances spiritual energies, aids mental concentration and encourages impartiality

HEALTH BENEFITS: relieves painful joints, treats ulcers and wounds, alleviates colds and flu, heals blemishes and wrinkles

WHERE TO PLACE THE CRYSTAL: on your desk, in your pocket or bag, on your living room table

Aries people are very positive and action-orientated, and are known for their ability to get things done. Ruled by the assertive planet Mars, they are often aggressive and can be considered "pushy." They are competitive, dynamic people and are often leaders in their chosen field of business. On the downside, Arians can be prone to bullying people weaker than themselves and can get easily bored and impatient.

♈ Aries

March 21–April 20

Ruling planet: **Mars**

Element: **Fire**

Birthstones: **diamond, ruby**

Related crystals: **amethyst, aquamarine, aventurine, citrine, garnet, jasper, topaz**

Crystal healing

One of the major weaknesses of Arians is their tendency to act in a reckless or rebellious manner, and this is where soothing crystal energies can be beneficial. So whenever you feel the inclination to act over-impulsively or make rash decisions, pick up your purple fluorite crystal and turn the stone over and over in your hand for about 5–10 minutes until the crystal's stabilizing vibrations make you feel more able to structure your thoughts constructively and to act in a more restrained and reasonable manner. Repeat as often as is necessary to calm you down.

In medical astrology Aries controls the head. Hold a red jasper crystal to your head to dispel any headaches that you get.

Realizing Arian ambitions with ruby

Cut and polished

Rough

Arians can be very impulsive people who are quick to assimilate facts, but they can find it hard to make big changes in their lives. They can be competitive and may try to get ahead in their career or to be good at a sport. They are born leaders and are often positive and outspoken. Even when they seem to be quite meek and mild, there is always an aggressive streak lurking somewhere in their psyche.

Crystal healing

Arians are generally cheerful and helpful people, and generally do not have a devious or sly side. Their assertive side often needs channeling into positive actions to achieve ambitions. So when you recognize that you are procrastinating about a desired aim, pick up and hold your ruby crystal in your hands for about 5 minutes and let the vibrations of this passionate stone give you the courage and determination to realize your aspiration.

CRYSTAL FACTS

CRYSTAL TO USE: ruby (red), opaque when uncut, transparent when polished

AVAILABILITY: commonly available when uncut

QUALITIES OF STONE: brings courage and integrity, aids strong leadership, helps motivation and realizing attainable ambitions

HEALTH BENEFITS: increases blood circulation, releases toxins, helps functioning of the adrenals, kidneys, and reproductive organs, stimulates brain functions, reduces fever

WHERE TO PLACE THE CRYSTAL: on your desk, in your pocket or bag, on your living room table

Diamond birthstone

The diamond symbolizes purity and it can help bring Arians' lives together. It can support their strong character by encouraging fearlessness, strength, and fortitude. It can also bring clarity, making them more considerate.

ALTERNATIVE ASPIRATIONAL CRYSTALS TO USE

Lepidolite: gives concentrated decision-making and focus

Agate: increases perception, boosts analytical functions (right: brown agate)

Removing Taurean inflexibility with natural quartz cluster

Rough with terminator

Taureans are very stable and dependable people that like consistency and order in their lives. They are patient and steadfast in their work and home life, but can also be very creative and often work in artistic professions. Ruled by Venus, the planet associated with the goddess of love, Taureans are very sensual and tactile people who have a sense of humor and enjoy the good things in life. However, their less attractive characteristics are stubbornness, inflexibility, laziness and a tendency to be opinionated.

CRYSTAL FACTS

CRYSTAL TO USE: natural quartz cluster (clear), all sizes

AVAILABILITY: commonly available

QUALITIES OF STONE: amplifies energy, dispels resistance to change, and promotes mental adaptability

HEALTH BENEFITS: good for any condition, stimulates immune system, soothes burns

WHERE TO PLACE THE CRYSTAL: on your desk, in your pocket or bag, on your living room table

Crystal healing

One of worst traits of Taureans is a resistance to change of any sort. So when you feel unable to move on in your life, or make an important change, pick up your natural quartz cluster and hold in your hands for about 5–10 minutes and focus on the change you want to make. If you prefer, meditate on your problem while looking at your stone. As you sense the natural emissions of the crystal, notice how your anxiety about the forthcoming change melts away. Repeat this several times if your resistance is hard to shift.

Taurus

April 21–May 20

Ruling planet: **Venus**

Element: **Earth**

Birthstones: **emerald, topaz**

Related stones: **aquamarine, diamond, kunzite, lapis lazuli, malachite, rose quartz, tiger's eye**

In medical astrology Taurus controls the throat. Hold an aquamarine crystal to your throat to cure a sore throat.

Increasing Taurean creativity with bloodstone

Polished

CRYSTAL FACTS

CRYSTAL TO USE: bloodstone, also known as heliotrope, is a type of green jasper that contains red spots of iron oxide.

AVAILABILITY: commonly available

QUALITIES OF STONE: alleviates stress, encourages inner wisdom and altruism, strengthens intuition, and increases creativity and talent

HEALTH BENEFITS: purifies and strengthens blood circulation and releases toxins from kidneys, liver, and spleen, increases metabolism

WHERE TO PLACE THE CRYSTAL: on your desk, in pocket or bag, on living room table

Taureans tend to be materialistic and often worry about not having enough money; security and having pleasant objects around is very important to them. They love luxuries and can enjoy eating good food and drinking fine wines. They often like to have reasonable savings behind them to protect them from upsets or changes that they can find so hard to bear. Their artistic side often leads them into architecture, fashion, photography, publishing, or the restaurant trade.

Crystal healing

Taureans often have a very lazy side. They can work steadily in their professions but lack the imagination or risk-taking abilities to become very successful. If you recognize these limitations in yourself and often feel the need to stimulate your creative side, work regularly with your bloodstone to bring some motivation. Hold the stone to your Third eye chakra in the middle of your forehead for several minutes daily, sensing how the crystal's stimulating impulses are giving you more vitality, new ideas, and awakening your creative juices.

Emerald birthstone

The emerald is linked to Venus, Taurus' ruler. It is a stone that encourages successful relationships and loyalty, something that most Taureans desire. It encourages unconditional love but also stimulates their hedonistic and pleasure-loving side.

ALTERNATIVE CREATIVITY CRYSTALS TO USE

Lapis lazuli: brings self-awareness, helps express new ideas

Citrine: raises self-confidence, opens creative side

Kunzite: encourages self-expression and creativity

Citrine to give Geminis more patience

Geminis are great talkers. They have a versatile intellect and inquiring minds, and their charm can help them through difficult situations. Ruled by Mercury, the planet of communication, they love conversation but their restless personality is always observing what else is going on around them. Their less admirable traits are self-involvement, a lack of attention to detail, obsessiveness, and a tendency to feel the grass is always greener somewhere else.

Crystal healing

A less attractive side of Geminis is their impatience in dealing with life situations, or keeping their attention focused on what is happening, or listening to a person's replies. So when you can feel yourself drifting off into middle distance in an important conversation, take hold of your citrine crystal and clutch it tightly until you feel the crystal working with you, helping your concentration to return, giving you the ability to respond in a reasoned and interested way. Use whenever you feel restless or distracted.

Cluster

CRYSTAL FACTS

CRYSTAL TO USE: citrine (yellow, yellow/brown), transparent, often a cluster

AVAILABILITY: natural citrine can be hard to find; citrine produced by heat-treating amethyst is commonly available

QUALITIES OF STONE: strengthens concentration, encourages inner calm and the ability to be more analytical

HEALTH BENEFITS: assists eye problems, detoxifies the blood, relieves digestive upsets, helps menopausal problems such as hot flashes and tiredness

WHERE TO PLACE THE CRYSTAL: on your desk, in your pocket or bag, on your living room table

 *Gemini*

May 21–June 20

Ruling planet: **Mercury**

Element: **Air**

Birthstones: **agate, tiger's eye, tourmaline**

Related crystals: **aquamarine, calcite, chrysocolla, citrine, rutilated quartz, sapphire, topaz**

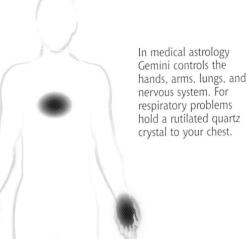

In medical astrology Gemini controls the hands, arms, lungs, and nervous system. For respiratory problems hold a rutilated quartz crystal to your chest.

Soothing Gemini nerves with turquoise

Geminis love to be on the go. They have a lot of energy and often want to do everything at once. They love a variety of tasks in their work to keep their interest, and they welcome the opportunity to meet new people; stable, routine jobs do not interest them at all. Mentally they are always looking to the next project they can tackle; with their inquisitive mentality the future is always more attractive. They can at times upset friends and family with some emotionless or thoughtless actions to get what they want.

Crystal healing

Trying to achieve so much in their daily lives can create regular nervous tension for Geminis; many live on their nerves. So if you live with this constant tension in your life, work with your turquoise stone to bring some inner peace. When you start to feel agitated and sense your nervous system becoming frayed, pick up your turquoise crystal and place it on your Solar plexus chakra in your upper abdomen. Breathe deeply from your diaphragm and let the healing energies calm your nervous system until you feel nerves in control once again. Use the stone whenever events start to overwhelm you.

Polished

CRYSTAL FACTS

CRYSTAL TO USE: turquoise (green or blue), opaque, often with veins, generally polished

AVAILABILITY: commonly available

QUALITIES OF STONE: helps creative expression, balances emotions, prevents mood swings, calms the nerves

HEALTH BENEFITS: revitalizes blood circulation, regenerates tissue, aids viral infections, soothes cramps and pain

WHERE TO PLACE THE CRYSTAL: on your desk, in your pocket or bag, on your living room table

Agate birthstone

A grounding stone, agate enhances mental function. It can help to focus Geminis, helping them to study the necessary details to understand the full complexities of a situation.

ALTERNATIVE CALMING CRYSTAL TO USE

Magnesite: reduces emotional stress, intolerance, and nervous tension

Balancing Cancerian moods with rose quartz

Cancerians are very family-orientated. They love security and their homes, and they like to feel they belong. They are protective and caring people. Ruled by the Moon, which is linked to emotions, they are sensitive and intuitive and are often good at jobs that involve helping the public in some way. They are hard-working and can make good politicians. One of the less attractive sides to their characters is their moodiness. They can also be self-pitying and clingy and can have an inferiority complex.

Rough

Crystal healing

People who have Cancerians as friends often complain of their regular emotional upsets, and how moody and secretive they can be. So when you start to feel a bit emotionally unbalanced or can feel a sulk coming on, take out your rose quartz crystal and hold it to your heart for about 5 minutes. Let its pure loving vibrations soothe and regulate your mood, filling you with joy and a positive attitude. Use your stone again whenever you start to feel upset or want to withdraw.

CRYSTAL FACTS

CRYSTAL TO USE: rose quartz (pink), normally translucent, can be tumbled

AVAILABILITY: commonly available

QUALITIES OF STONE: emotional healer and balancer, clears resentment, increases love of self, promotes forgiveness

HEALTH BENEFITS: releases toxins from body, increases fertility, soothes burns, aids the complexion, relieves respiratory problems

WHERE TO PLACE THE CRYSTAL: on your desk, in your pocket or bag, on your living room table

Cancer

June 21–July 22

Ruling planet: **Moon**

Element: **Water**

Birthstones: **moonstone, pearl, ruby**

Related crystals: **amber, aventurine, chrysoprase emerald, moss agate, rhodochrosite**

In medical astrology Cancer controls the breasts, stomach, and reproductive system. To relieve stomach ache hold an agate crystal to your abdomen.

Promoting Cancerian security with moonstone

Cancerians live on their emotions. They are great worriers, often concerning themselves about events that never happen. They are great nurturers and homemakers and can excel at cooking. Their heightened sensitivity to people's moods can sometimes make them feel resentful or a victim.

Pearl birthstone

In ancient legends pearls were the tears of the gods. This stone helps to balance a Cancerian's erratic emotions and soothes the Heart chakra. It attracts love and can give courage, attributes that this sign can lack.

Crystal healing

As they worry so much, Cancerians can feel concerned about the future or cling to the past. Often acting in an unsettled, rather helpless manner, they can need a lot of reassurance from the people close to them. If you are aware you can turn these emotions into something positive even as you fight against them. Use moonstone to smooth out your moods, encourage more stability, and heal your stress. When you start to feel insecure and upset, pick up your moonstone and hold it to your Solar plexus chakra in your upper abdomen for several minutes and feel how this caring stone starts to balance your emotions, making you feel safe and protected once more. Use the crystal whenever you start to feel tearful or upset. Avoid working with the stone during a full moon as the effects can be too strong.

CRYSTAL FACTS

CRYSTAL TO USE: moonstone (white, cream, yellow, blue, green), cloudy and translucent

AVAILABILITY: commonly available

QUALITIES OF STONE: calms overemotional or sharp reactions, soothes and stabilizes and helps to dissolve old, unhelpful patterns

HEALTH BENEFITS: encourages release of waste products, balances PMS symptoms, helps reduce swellings, aids digestion and reproductive organs

WHERE TO PLACE THE CRYSTAL: on your desk, in your pocket or bag, on your living room table

Polished

ALTERNATIVE SECURITY CRYSTALS TO USE

Agate: a grounding stone that brings emotional balance (right: green moss agate)

Chrysoprase: brings emotional security and trust

Amazonite: soothes any emotional worries and fears

Calming Leo's over exuberance with watermelon tourmaline

Rough

CRYSTAL FACTS

CRYSTAL TO USE: watermelon tourmaline (green and pink), opaque or transparent, often long and a hexagonal shape

AVAILABILITY: commonly available

QUALITIES OF STONE: instills patience, encourages more tact and diplomacy, dispels old emotional pain and fears

HEALTH BENEFITS: regulates nervous system, reduces stress, treats lymphatic disease

WHERE TO PLACE THE CRYSTAL: on your desk, in your pocket or handbag, on your living room table

In medical astrology Leo controls the heart and spine. Hold a carnelian crystal to your lower back to relieve backache.

Leos love to bask in people's admiration and to be the center of attention. They like to be noticed and often wear dramatic clothing or jewelry to stand out. Ruled by the Sun, which is linked to the ego, they tend to be successful in business and are often figures of authority. They are generous, good-hearted people who look after their families. The less likable characteristics of Leos are their tendencies to be domineering, arrogant, self-centered, and overbearing.

Leo

July 23–August 22

Ruling planet: **Sun**

Element: **Fire**

Birthstones: **garnet, ruby, tiger's eye**

Related crystals: **amber, carnelian, fire agate, golden beryl (heliodor), onyx, peridot**

Crystal healing

Leos generally have happy, sunny personalities and will brighten any room they enter. But they can be have tendency to bask in their own glory and to be hedonistic, demanding, and self-righteous. If you recognize that you can be overexuberant or overwhelming in certain situations, calm yourself down by privately taking out your watermelon tourmaline crystal. Hold it tightly in your hands until you feel the stone's balancing energies encouraging you to listen and be more diplomatic and sensitive in what you are saying. Use your crystal whenever you feel yourself becoming unrealistic or too demanding.

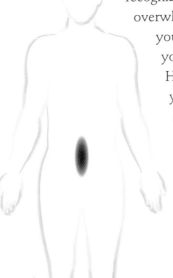

Increasing Leo's self-worth with tiger's eye

Polished red tiger's eye

Leos are life's realists and their optimistic personalities help them to recover from problems and look forward to the future. Their natural ability to project light and warmth wherever they go needs to be controlled, however, as their egos can take over and they can fail to see their own shortcomings. People can also be confused by the supposed self-assurance of Leos— deep down they need to be needed, and they want, above all, to be loved and appreciated.

Crystal healing

Beneath their outgoing and self-possessed exteriors many Leos lack self-confidence and can be very vulnerable to criticism. There is a need to feel that they "count" in the world. If you regularly suffer from a lack of self-worth or want to recover from an upsetting verbal attack, pick up your tiger's eye crystal and hold it on your Sacral chakra in the lower abdomen for several minutes, feeling how the stone's supportive emanations help to resolve any dilemmas and inner conflicts, and rebuild your feelings of self-worth. Regularly use the stone to release any bitterness and frustration.

CRYSTAL FACTS

CRYSTAL TO USE: tiger's eye (browny yellow, blue, red), banded appearance, often tumbled

AVAILABILITY: commonly available

QUALITIES OF STONE: gives insight into your own shortcomings, increases personal power, heals any self-criticism

HEALTH BENEFITS: aids asthma, helps digestive system, heals throat infections

WHERE TO PLACE THE CRYSTAL: on your desk, in your pocket or bag, on your living room table

Ruby birthstone

Ruby is a passionate stone that can increase the generous spirit and overall enthusiasm of the Leo personality. Its dynamic qualities work positively to encourage the best of a Leo's natural leadership abilities.

ALTERNATIVE CONFIDENCE-BUILDING CRYSTALS TO USE

Hematite: boosts self-esteem and gives confidence

Sodalite: releases fears and enhances self-acceptance

Alleviating Virgo's obsessive tendencies with ocean jasper

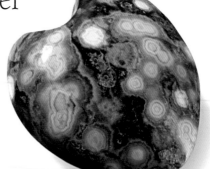

Polished heart

Virgoans are very practical people. They love to be well organized and are efficient in their work and all the tasks they undertake. They are seekers of information, both in the world around them and also in their own lives, and excel in jobs such as accountancy, the media, IT, or marketing. Ruled by Mercury, the planet of communication and logical behavior, Virgoans are very analytical in their approach to life and love, establishing well-run systems. Their unappealing characteristics include being stubborn, sarcastic, pedantic, and testy and feeling undervalued.

Virgo

August 23–September 22

Ruling planet: **Mercury**

Element: **Earth**

Birthstones: **carnelian, peridot, sapphire**

Related crystals: **amazonite, citrine, jade, moss agate, opal, rose quartz**

In medical astrology Virgo controls the nervous system and the intestines. To calm your nerves hold a smoky quartz crystal to your abdomen.

Crystal healing

An irritating aspect of the Virgoan personality is a tendency to be obsessed about their health, worrying about every minor ache and pain. When you sense you are being a hypochondriac, take hold of your ocean jasper crystal and place it on your skin to let its nurturing vibrations work through your body, removing any negative energies, soothing your anxiety, and releasing your obsessive worries. Use your crystal whenever you start to panic about the state of your health.

CRYSTAL FACTS

CRYSTAL TO USE: ocean jasper, opaque, patterned, often tumbled

AVAILABILITY: commonly available

QUALITIES OF STONE: balances and releases obsessive inclinations, nurtures and supports during stress, absorbs negative energy

HEALTH BENEFITS: strengthens liver, gall bladder, circulatory and digestive systems, relieves stomach upsets

WHERE TO PLACE THE CRYSTAL: on your desk, in your pocket or bag, on your living room table

Rising above Virgoan irritation with rhodochrosite

Work is important to Virgoans; they like having a good position and being appreciated for their competency. If they have to fight their corner, they can become despondent and lose confidence in themselves. This in turn can make them whine about how no one appreciates them. They get bored easily and need the excitement of taking up many interests, but do not always follow them through.

Peridot birthstone

This visionary stone increases aware-ness of the hidden detail of different situations, so works well with Virgoans who love to get to the heart of the matter. It also sharpens their minds, bringing increased understanding.

Crystal healing

Virgoans are true perfectionists and when life does not match up to their expectations they can become very irritable. So when your nerves feel frayed, pick up your pink, compassionate rhodochrosite crystal to balance your emotional state. Hold it over your heart and chest for several minutes until you feel your breathing and heartbeat slowing and your frustration and tension releasing. Take hold of your stone whenever you feel you are starting to lose patience.

Polished

CRYSTAL FACTS

CRYSTAL TO USE: rhodochrosite (pinky), banded, can be polished or tumbled

AVAILABILITY: commonly available

QUALITIES OF STONE: emotional balancer, helps confront unreasonable fears, lifts depression, and encourages a positive attitude

HEALTH BENEFITS: aids the kidneys and heart, increases blood circulation, relieves asthma and breathing problems, alleviates migraines, boosts the thryroid

WHERE TO PLACE THE CRYSTAL: on your desk, in your pocket or bag, on your living room table

ALTERNATIVE IRRITATION-RELIEVING CRYSTALS TO USE

Blue apatite: alleviates irritability and emotional exhaustion

Aventurine: calms irritation, promotes feelings of wellbeing

Lavender (purple) jade: encourages emotional release, reduces irritability

Balancing Libra's critical side with aquamarine

Polished

CRYSTAL FACTS

CRYSTAL TO USE: aquamarine (greeny blue), clear/opaque, often tumbled

AVAILABILITY: commonly available

QUALITIES OF STONE: overcomes intolerance of others, helps creative expression, calms nerves and mental confusion, increases sensitivity

HEALTH BENEFITS: alleviates fluid retention, relieves sore throats, swollen glands, acts as a general tonic, reduces hay fever

WHERE TO PLACE THE CRYSTAL: on your desk, in your pocket or handbag, on your living room table

Librans like harmony in their lives, and often seek fairness and balance in everything they attempt. They have pleasant personalities and can mix well at a party, although they can have a tendency to forget the people they have met. Ruled by Venus, the goddess of love and pleasure, Librans like easy going relationships. They have a great love of beauty and need to live in pleasant surroundings. The characteristics that are not so appealing are being indecisive and insincere, lacking self-reliance, and being superficial and vain.

Crystal healing

Another Libran flaw is the habit of being overcritical. They can get very exasperated about other people's faults and their inability to correct them. If you recognize this trait as part of your personality, take out your aquamarine crystal when you feel you are just about to criticize someone, and hold it for a few minutes to your throat. Sense how its supportive vibrations are calming you down, dispersing your judgmental attitudes, and bringing some much-needed tolerance. Use your crystal whenever you feel your sharp tongue is coming into action.

In medical astrology Libra controls the kidneys, bladder, and buttocks. To mitigate a bladder infection, hold a bloodstone crystal to the area.

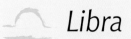

Libra

September 23–October 22

Ruling planet: **Venus**

Element: **Air**

Birthstones: **chrysoprase, opal, sapphire**

Related crystals: **aquamarine, aventurine, emerald, opal, peridot, smoky quartz**

Boosting Libran good feelings with chrysoprase

Librans have a sense of fair play and can make great arbitrators and administrators. They like to be part of a team as they can find decision-making hard work. They like beautiful objects so can be drawn toward design and creative careers. They have a tendency to be in another space mentally, to have "their heads in the clouds," and often need to be grounded or brought back to reality.

Polished

Crystal healing

Librans normally have an easygoing personality but can also be prone to moodiness and depression. So if you know that you can feel a bit low at times, hold your chrysoprase to your forehead and allow this serene stone to bring you joy and happiness, letting you enjoy simple things once again. Hold the stone for several minutes and feel its vibrational power lifting your mood and making you feel ready to enjoy a basic pleasure such as a walk by the river or sitting in the sun in your local park. Use the stone whenever you feel yourself becoming depressed.

Sapphire birthstone

Librans love beauty of all kinds so they feel an affinity with this serene stone that promotes harmony and balance. A white sapphire supports their belief in fair play and justice for all.

CRYSTAL FACTS

CRYSTAL TO USE: chrysoprase (green, lemon/yellow), opaque, flecked, often tumbled

AVAILABILITY: commonly available

QUALITIES OF STONE: encourages creativity, stimulates self-acceptance, brings a sense of security and trust, helps when taking on new projects

HEALTH BENEFITS: relieves depression, increases fertility, eases sexual frustration, aids relaxation and good sleep, alleviates skin disease

WHERE TO PLACE THE CRYSTAL: on your desk, in your pocket or bag, on your living room table

ALTERNATIVE MOOD-LIFTING CRYSTALS TO USE

Jet: balances mood swings, dispels depression

Turquoise: brings emotional balance, promotes wellbeing

Lapis lazuli: balances body and spirit, increases creativity and vitality

Bloodstone for banishing Scorpio possessiveness

Scorpios are intense, magnetic people who are courageous and passionate in everything they undertake. They are also very sensitive, with a well-developed intuition. Ruled by both assertive Mars and secretive Pluto, Scorpios are strong characters who are not always easy to live with or to work for. They love investigative work and are often drawn to professions such as medicine, psychiatry, or journalism. The less appealing side of their personalities is that they can hang on to resentments and be ruthless, suspicious, and have a jealous side.

Crystal healing

One of the least appealing characteristics of Scorpios is their tendency to be possessive with friends and lovers. So when you start to feel jealous because your partner is going out or perhaps resent that a friend is going on vacation without you, close your eyes and hold your bloodstone crystal firmly in your hands for about 5–10 minutes. Feel how its subtle vibrations start to calm your mind, promote selflessness, and release your clinging tendencies. Use the stone whenever you feel possessive.

Polished

CRYSTAL FACTS

CRYSTAL TO USE: bloodstone, also known as heliotrope, is a type of green jasper that contains red spots of iron oxide

AVAILABILITY: commonly available

QUALITIES OF STONE: reduces stress and revitalizes body and mind, heals psyche and inner conflict

HEALTH BENEFITS: increases blood circulation, detoxifies liver, kidneys, bladder, and spleen, stimulates the metabolism

WHERE TO PLACE THE CRYSTAL: on your desk, in your pocket or bag, on your living room table

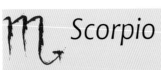

Scorpio

October 23–November 21

Ruling planets: **Pluto, Mars**

Element: **Water**

Birthstones: **aquamarine, malachite, topaz**

Related crystals: **dark opal, green tourmaline, herkimer diamond, obsidian, turquoise**

In medical astrology Scorpio controls the reproductive system, the bowels, and the bladder. For menstrual cramps hold a jet crystal to your abdomen.

Scorpios can learn forgiveness with apache tear obsidian

Scorpios are very emotional signs. They often make decisions emotionally through excitement or anger without always thinking things through. They generally have hot tempers and have a tendency to overreact to situations, often being mortally offended by something someone says, even if no disrespect was intended.

Crystal healing

As their emotions rule their lives, Scorpios can hold a grudge when a friend, colleague, or relative upsets them. They can brood for a long time over the altercation, finding it extremely difficult to get over what has happened, and can make bitter enemies. If you know you have these tendencies and find it hard to forgive and forget, use your apache tear obsidian stone after every upsetting confrontation. Hold the stone to your heart for several minutes daily for a week after the argument, feeling how the crystal is calming you down, encouraging your forgiveness, and working on dispelling the bitterness and distress that you are holding there.

Polished

CRYSTAL FACTS

CRYSTAL TO USE: apache tear obsidian (black), translucent

AVAILABILITY: commonly available

QUALITIES OF STONE: absorbs negative energies, shields the aura, releases deep-rooted grievances, promotes forgiveness

HEALTH BENEFITS: cleanses body of toxins, relieves muscle spasms

WHERE TO PLACE THE CRYSTAL: on your desk, in your pocket or bag, on your living room table

Malachite birthstone

Life is lived more powerfully under the influence of this stone, which suits the adventurous Scorpio perfectly. It promotes risk-taking and change for spiritual growth, and encourages unconditional love.

ALTERNATIVE FORGIVENESS CRYSTALS TO USE

Rutilated quartz: soothes black moods, promotes forgiveness

Rhodonite: eases emotional trauma, helps reconciliation and forgiveness

Topaz: healing stone that releases tension, encourages generosity, and aids forgiveness

Rough

CRYSTAL FACTS

CRYSTAL TO USE: Blue with gold flecks; may be blue and white (white is calcite); may have black spots of lazulite

AVAILABILITY: commonly available but expensive

QUALITIES OF STONE: gives mental clarity, promotes self-awareness and inner wisdom, increases psychic abilities, releases stress and tension

HEALTH BENEFITS: strengthens thyroid gland, relieves painful headaches, aids depression, cleanses organs and purifies blood, stabilizes blood pressure

WHERE TO PLACE THE CRYSTAL: on your desk, in your pocket or bag, on your living room table

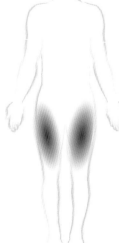

In medical astrology Sagittarius controls the hips and thighs. For a hip problem, treat it with jade.

Avoiding Sagittarian excessive behavior with lapis lazuli

Sagittarians can be very adventurous people as they love to travel, but they also have a conservative side and need a safe, secure haven to which they can return. They are normally cheerful people with an optimistic outlook on life. They are often drawn to publishing or the travel industry. Their wit or sense of humor works well in these professions. The downside of their personalities is the tendency to lose their temper or be tactless. They can also be too confident, boastful, or fixed in their views.

Crystal healing

One of the problems with Sagittarians is their tendency to act excessively, going all out to achieve a goal. If you feel yourself running out of steam trying to excel at a work project or trying to do too many things at once, pick up your lapis lazuli crystal and hold it firmly for about 5 minutes, or hold it to your forehead, feeling how this serene stone is calming your stress, increasing your inner wisdom, slowing you down, and bringing inner peace. Use the stone whenever you go into hyper-drive.

 Sagittarius

November 22–December 21

Ruling planet: **Jupiter**

Element: **Fire**

Birthstones: **sapphire, topaz, turquoise,**

Related crystals: **amethyst, blue lace agate, garnet, malachite, ruby, smoky quartz, sodalite**

Widening Sagittarians' vision with topaz

Polished

CRYSTAL FACTS

CRYSTAL TO USE: blue topaz, transparent, pointed, can be faceted

AVAILABILITY: readily available from specialist stores

QUALITIES OF STONE: aids self-expression and creativity, gives clarity, promotes forgiveness, supports positive thoughts and affirmations, helps to achieve own desires

HEALTH BENEFITS: strengthens thyroid gland, regenerates tissue, relieves throat disorders, helps good digestion

WHERE TO PLACE THE CRYSTAL: on your desk, in your pocket or handbag, on your living room table

Sagittarians can be quite altruistic and can burden themselves with society's problems. They like helping others and can end up helping out down-at-luck friends or relatives. The philosophizing "putting the world to rights" side of some Sagittarians can be at odds with their more earthly desires to socialize and to party. Their adventurous personality seeks a merging of their spiritual and physical desires.

Turquoise birthstone

The stabilizing quality of turquoise can bring some calm to this fiery sign when they are going all out for a goal. Mentally it can help with problem-solving and can relieve exhaustion caused by the Sagittarian tendency to overwork.

Crystal healing

Sagittarians are often uninterested in money and can spend a large proportion of their lives on a spiritual quest. Sometimes their aspirations are unrealistic or impractical and they need to be brought back down to earth. If you know that you regularly pursue causes or projects that have little foundation, spend some time working with your blue topaz crystal and let its inspiring rays give a new perspective to what you are trying to do and show a way forward. Hold the stone to your Third eye chakra in the middle of your forehead whenever you have lost your way, and let its vibrant energy move you in a new direction, giving you the light to find the right and true path.

ALTERNATIVE VISION-SEEKING CRYSTALS TO USE

Diamond: stimulates imagination, aids spiritual aspirations

Pietersite: encourages inner guidance and removes spiritual fantasies

Polished

CRYSTAL FACTS

CRYSTAL TO USE: chalcedony

AVAILABILITY: commonly available, but can be expensive

QUALITIES OF STONE: encourages optimism and goodwill, lifts mood and brings joy, dispels self-doubt, brings a benevolent attitude

HEALTH BENEFITS: improves blood circulation and the functioning of the spleen, bone marrow, and gall bladder, increases physical energy

WHERE TO PLACE THE CRYSTAL: on your desk, in your pocket or bag, on your living room table

Dispelling Capricorn depression with chalcedony

Capricorns are very sensible and capable people. They are hard-working and ambitious and like a structured lifestyle. Ruled by Saturn, the teacher of the zodiac, they can be affected by the restrictions, struggles, and attention to detail that this serious planet demands. They can be addicted to work and are often found working in industries such as banking and accounting, but may also be self-employed. The less attractive side of Capricorns is their meanness or pettiness, inflexibility, and tendencies to be aloof and to use other people to further their own gains.

Capricorn

December 22–January 19

Ruling planet: **Saturn**

Element: **Earth**

Birthstones: **garnet, jet, onyx**

Related crystals: **amethyst, moonstone, moss agate, obsidian, peridot, ruby, sugilite**

Crystal healing

One of the unappealing characteristics of Capricorns is their predisposition to be depressed: they can be melancholic or wallow in their own misery. So if you recognize that you regularly feel sorry for yourself, take hold of your chalcedony crystal when your mood deteriorates and hold it in your hands or to your Third eye chakra in the middle of your forehead. Let its nurturing vibrations lift your melancholy and give you back your optimism and enjoyment of life. Use your crystal whenever your emotions take a downturn.

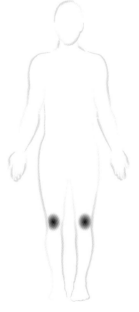

In medical astrology Capricorn controls the body's skeleton, knees, and skin. For knee problems use an azurite crystal.

Capricorns can learn to cope under presssure with yellow jasper

Capricorns can suffer from insecurity, and even when they have savings and a good job they can worry about becoming impoverished. They can be reasonable and caring people but can also possess a hot temper. Many Capricorns suffer from a lack of self-esteem and need to feel valued and have their efforts appreciated, particularly at work. They can seem old at a young age, only becoming more comfortable with themselves and their families as they establish themselves at work and grow older.

Polished

Onyx birthstone

Onyx is a vigorous and strong stone that can support the serious, hardworking and ambitious side of Capricorns. It can also bolster their self-confidence, which is often lacking, despite their abilities.

Crystal healing

Capricorns are very reliable people and often take care of family members. As they are so competent in many areas of their lives, they are seen as totally dependable and many people can lean on them. If you often find the pressure of helping people is getting too much, or you are constantly at the beck and call of your family, pick up your yellow jasper crystal and clasp it in your hands or place it on your Solar plexus chakra in your upper abdomen. Focus on what you want to balance in your life and let the stone's nurturing qualities give you the energy and stamina you need to cope.

CRYSTAL FACTS

CRYSTAL TO USE: yellow jasper

AVAILABILITY: commonly available

QUALITIES OF STONE: quietens the nerves, encourages balance, supports when under stress, protects you from, and dispels negative energies, aids quick thinking and organizational skills

HEALTH BENEFITS: relieves nausea, bladder, and stomach problems, supports the circulatory system, promotes the release of toxins

WHERE TO PLACE THE CRYSTAL: on your desk, in your pocket or bag, on your living room table

ALTERNATIVE COPING CRYSTALS TO USE

Amethyst: balances emotional highs and lows, dispels anxiety

Chrysoprase: brings solutions to situations, encourages positive thinking

Celestite: alleviates worries, promotes mental clarity

Reducing Aquarians' impulsive action with aventurine

Polished

CRYSTAL FACTS

CRYSTAL TO USE: aventurine (green, blue, red, brown, pale orange)

AVAILABILITY: commonly available

QUALITIES OF STONE: dispels anxiety and fear, encourages calmness and tranquillity, increases perception and creativity, brings empathy and compassion

HEALTH BENEFITS: improves blood flow, balances blood pressure, lowers cholesterol, improves skin complaints, eases migraines, relieves eye problems

WHERE TO PLACE THE CRYSTAL: on your desk, in your pocket or handbag, on your living room table

Aquarians are logical, intelligent people who like to work out problems analytically. They can have a big circle of friends but may find it hard to maintain a one-to-one, intimate relationship, as they are often more emotionally detached and like their own independence. Ruled by Uranus, the planet of ideals, and Saturn, planet of restriction and limitations, they can be humanitarian but often hang onto fixed ideas. Negatively, Aquarians can be self-centered, pedantic, reluctant to compromise, and inflexible in their attitudes.

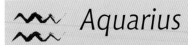

Aquarius

January 20–February 17

Ruling planet: **Saturn, Uranus**

Element: **Air**

Birthstones: **amethyst, aquamarine, kunzite**

Related crystals: **agate, blue celestite, chrysoprase, garnet, moonstone, natural quartz, turquoise**

Crystal healing

Another unfavorable side of Aquarians is their lack of sympathy or empathy for people. They find it hard to be supportive when someone is ill. If you start to get irritated by a person's negativity or you cannot cope when they are complaining about their problems, pick up your aventurine crystal. Hold it to your Heart chakra in the middle of your chest and feel its compassionate pulsations opening up your caring and loving side. Use the stone whenever you lack a positive emotional response.

In medical astrology Aquarius controls the calves and ankles. For leg cramps use a hematite crystal.

Cluster

CRYSTAL FACTS

CRYSTAL TO USE: amethyst (violet/purple), transparent, geode, cluster or polished

AVAILABILITY: very commonly available

QUALITIES OF STONE: heals mind and emotions, relieves depression, calms or stimulates mind when needed, helps practical decision-making, alleviates stress and tension

HEALTH BENEFITS: cleanses the blood, strengthens the immune and endocrine systems, relieves headaches and tension, soothes bruises and swellings

WHERE TO PLACE THE CRYSTAL: on your desk, in your pocket or bag, on your living room table

Aquarians take on new ideas with amethyst

Aquarians can be quite eccentric, individualistic people, who are often interested in New Age subjects. They can be competitive in their field of work, but can also be drawn to the caring professions, teaching, or IT, which particularly suits their logical minds. Although Aquarians crave their own space and despise clingy relationships, they are a fixed sign and stay for a long time in a job or relationship, when they have committed to someone. However, if they decide to leave, their decision can be quite cold and clinical.

Crystal healing

The logical Aquarian brain is very versatile, and being with an Aquarian is never boring. However, they do have a tendency to hang onto their fixed views and be reluctant to change their way of life. If you have problems embracing new ideas or projects and feel frustrated that you find it hard to make changes, take your amethyst crystal in your hand or place it on the crown of your head. Close your eyes, and let its soothing energies bring insight and increase your perceptiveness into how you can make changes in your life.

Aquamarine birthstone

Aquarians have very sharp brains and working with aquamarine can help them filter information and gain extra perceptive skills. It also increases feelings of sensitivity, which can aid Aquarians as they can be rather unemotional.

ALTERNATIVE CHANGE CRYSTALS TO USE

Bloodstone: assists adjustment to change

Blue chalcedony: opens the mind to new ideas

Chrysocolla: allows acceptance of change

Overcoming Piscean mood swings with aragonite

Pisceans are sensitive people with a well-developed intuition. They are often spiritually enlightened and may seem to live with their heads in the clouds. Ruled by Neptune, the planet of dreams and illusions, and by Jupiter, the planet of good luck and opportunity, Pisceans can be very altruistic, dreamy, and kind people. At their worst they can be indecisive, and can sink into chaos, become very depressed, and be emotionally unpredictable.

CRYSTAL FACTS

CRYSTAL TO USE: aragonite (white, yellow, gold, green, blue, brown) often translucent with spiky protusions

AVAILABILITY: commonly available

QUALITIES OF STONE: encourages mental discipline, gives insight to problems, grounds and centers the emotions, helps concentration, bring tolerance

HEALTH BENEFITS: strengthens bone structure, pain reliever, aids muscles spasms, boosts immune system

WHERE TO PLACE THE CRYSTAL: on your desk, in your pocket or handbag, on your living room table

Crystal healing

One of the less endearing sides of Pisceans is their moodiness. Because of their sensitivity to what is going on around them, they can soak up a person's unhappiness and become easily upset. So if you sense your mood deteriorating, pick up your grounding aragonite crystal and hold it in your hands or over your Third eye chakra in the middle of your forehead. Let this healing stone soothe and release your emotional stress and balance your sensitivity. Use your crystal whenever your mood takes a downward turn.

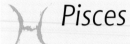

Pisces

February 18–March 20

Ruling planets: **Neptune, Jupiter**

Element: **Water**

Birthstones: **amethyst, black opal, moonstone**

Related crystals: **beryl, bloodstone, blue lace agate, chrysoprase, tourmaline, turquoise**

In medical astrology Pisces controls the feet. If you have foot problems use an onyx crystal.

Cluster

Pisces can foster realistic dreams with smoky quartz

Pisceans love the arts and are often into music, painting, dance, and work in creative industries such as photography and publishing. However, they can often be impractical at home. There can be an innocence about Pisceans, and many never truly grow up, sometimes feeling more at home with children or animals.

Rough

Crystal healing

Pisceans can suffer from self-doubt and worry about the future. They can find it hard to come back down to earth enough to put some of their dreams into practice. If you know that you have a tendency to be on another plane and are often unrealistic about some of your aims, use smoky quartz regularly to focus on what is possible. Hold it to your Root chakra in your lower abdomen for several minutes and feel its grounding emissions clearing your mind, giving you the guidance to follow an attainable dream.

CRYSTAL FACTS

RYSTAL TO USE: smoky quartz (brown/black), translucent and pointed, can be irradiated

AVAILABILITY: commonly available, but check that it is smoky quartz

QUALITIES OF STONE: lifts depression, balances emotions, very grounding, lessens fear, promotes positive thoughts. Clears subconscious blocks, helps realize your dreams

HEALTH BENEFITS: strengthens adrenal glands and kidneys, boosts energy, increases fertility, alleviates pain and headaches, supports the back and nervous system

WHERE TO PLACE THE CRYSTAL: on your desk, in your pocket or bag, on your living room table

Polished

Moonstone birthstone

A moonstone links to the moon's cycles and intuition, so it can increase a Piscean's intuitive side and increase their awareness of inner feelings or messages. It can also soothe emotional instability,

ALTERNATIVE MANIFESTATION CRYSTALS TO USE

Rhodochrosite: gives a positive attitude, helps you choose the right aim

Golden beryl (heliodor): encourages initiative and aids helps turn an idea into reality

Cluster

CRYSTAL FACTS

WHERE TO BUY: ideally in a crystal shop, alternatively by mail order or the internet

CRYSTAL VIBRATIONS: crystals transmit energy fields and will communicate with you; their energy will feel good or not right for you

QUALITY OF CRYSTAL: check for a crystal with a strong color— e.g., if amethyst is not bright purple, its energy has faded; avoid any stones with chips or indentations

MOVING ON: crystals sometimes do their work and move on; you may lose one or want to give it to someone else. Let it go freely, knowing that another one will replace it

WATCH OUT FOR: dyed crystals. Many agates are dyed blue, green, and purple, which alters their energy; turquoise may be dyed howlite (blue howlite) with no flecks of gold; amber may be plastic (rub it against your thumb: it should feel waxy)

How to choose your crystals

Make going out to buy your first crystals a special time. Ideally take half a day or at least a few hours and visit a recommended crystal shop that stocks a wide range of crystals. Ask the owner questions about the crystals: a good shop will sell few dyed crystals. Lose yourself in the beauty and power of this vast array of delightful, colored stones, and remember that a crystal normally chooses you.

Finding your crystals

Make a list before your visit of the stones you need to work on the tips you want to do in the book. Wander around the store, stopping to pick up any crystals that appeal. When you are used to the energetics of the place, go to choose your first crystal. Check whether you want a rough or polished stone, a cluster or one with a terminated point.

• Now stand in front of the first tray of crystals, close your eyes, then open them and see which crystal catches your eye and says "pick me up."

• Hold the crystal in your hands and see if your hands get warm or start to tingle.

• Tune into your senses and see if you feel a surge of energy, a vibration, a humming, or can see light coming from the stone.

• If nothing occurs or it does not feel right, try another one—the best stone for you is the one that produces the strongest sensation.

Polished agate hearts

Work through your whole crystal list using this technique, but remember always follow your intuition: it is invariably right.

Green moss agate

Cleansing crystals in water

Crystals take in energy from their surroundings and people, so when you buy one from a shop it will still contain the energetic imprint of everyone who has handled it. So before you can use it for its chosen purpose, you need to cleanse it so that it will work at its highest vibration. Once crystals are in place at home or in the workplace, or if you wear crystal jewelry, they need cleansing weekly or monthly. If you are using a crystal for a healing purpose, cleanse it after each session or daily, as the stone will absorb the negative vibrations of the illness or emotional upset.

The water method

One of the simplest cleansing methods when you first buy a crystal and do not know its history is to soak it in a glass bowl of still spring water for 24 hours to remove any deeply embedded negativity. To cleanse normally, hold the crystal or piece of jewelry under running water in your kitchen sink for a few minutes, holding the intention to remove negativity and to bring it back to a neutral state. Dry thoroughly after both methods.

CRYSTAL FACTS

WHAT CLEANSER TO USE: spring water

QUALITIES OF CLEANSER: water: a ritual purifier that removes negativity

CRYSTALS NOT TO CLEANSE IN WATER: selenite, lapis lazuli, malachite, turquoise. These stones are either water-soluble or the physical properties are affected by the water

Aqua aura

Polished snowflake obsidian

Cleansing crystals in saltwater

There are many different views and crystal traditions when it comes to saltwater cleansing. Some crystal healers do not recommend it as they feel it is too harsh a technique for crystals; others take the scientific approach—when an electrical charge is introduced to saltwater by the addition of a crystal, a battery effect is set up which will effectively "run down" the crystal's energy.

Polished pietersite

The saltwater method

Salt, however, has been used for thousands of years as a wonderful, natural purifier, for physical healing and in sacred cleansing ceremonies. If you want to try this method, place a handful of sea salt in a glass bowl filled with spring water. Let the salt dissolve completely before immersing the crystal, as the salt can scratch a soft stone. Hold the intention to remove all negativity. Leave for an hour, then rinse the crystal in pure spring water before drying. If you feel your crystals aren't working well using this method, then choose one of the other methods suggested.

CRYSTAL FACTS

WHAT CLEANSER TO USE: spring water with sea salt added

QUALITIES OF CLEANSER: water: a ritual purifier that removes negativity; salt: ancient purifying ingredient with antiseptic qualities

CRYSTALS NOT TO CLEANSE IN WATER OR SALTWATER: selenite, lapis lazuli, malachite, turquoise. These stones are either water-soluble or the physical properties are affected by the water

CRYSTALS NOT TO CLEANSE IN SALTWATER: calcite, carnelian, labradorite, opal, as it changes their physical properties

Rough blue tourmaline

Polished danburite

Cleansing crystals by smudging

Smudging is an ancient tradition that clears a space of any unpleasant sensations or negative energies. Smudge sticks are made from rolled-up dried herbs and when lit produce a cleansing smoke. Sage is one of the most powerful purifiers, and its healing smoke can effectively cleanse your crystals of negative vibrations. It is particularly good for crystal jewelry.

Smudge sticks

The smudging method

To cleanse a new crystal or jewelry, or several, place them in a bowl. Light your smudge stick, holding it over a fireproof bowl, blow out the flame, and then waft the smoke over your crystal several times to remove negativity and bring its vibrancy back to normal. This purifying method can also cleanse you and the room. Rinse under the faucet to extinguish. Incense is less powerful than smudging but can purify one crystal at a time. Light your incense stick, and when it is smoldering, gently waft the smoke over the crystal a few times, then leave to burn out on the holder.

CRYSTAL FACTS

WHAT CLEANSER TO USE: a sage smudge stick or, if unavailable, a frankincense incense stick

QUALITIES OF CLEANSER: sage smudge stick: a powerful cleanser that removes psychic debris, negative influences or energies; frankincense incense stick: purifies crystals and is spiritually uplifting

Cleansing with a singing bowl

Metal singing bowls have been used in the East for centuries for healing and to aid meditation. Made from seven metals, they are commonly used today in the West by therapists to raise energy levels. They are effective cleansers, and the humming sound they make when stroked can purify and lift the vibrancy of crystals.

The singing bowl method

Place the crystal, or several together, in the singing bowl and start to stroke the bowl's mallet around the inner or outer edge of the bowl and feel the sound building up. As you move the mallet in faster circles, negative energy from the crystals whirls away and brighter, positive energy is pulled in. Slowly stop playing the bowl and remove the crystals.

CRYSTAL FACTS

WHAT CLEANSER TO USE: metal Nepalese or Tibetan singing bowl

QUALITIES OF CLEANSER: a singing bowl creates a sound vibration that dispels negativity

CRYSTALS NOT TO CLEANSE BY SINGING BOWL: terminated crystals (with a point) as they can chip when moving around the bowl

Polished quartz, smoky quartz, and rose quartz with singing bowl

Cleansing by breath

When you have used a crystal for a quick healing treatment and are not able to use one of the more powerful cleansing methods detailed (see pages 149–150), perhaps if you are away from home and cannot easily use water, smudging, or the other cleansing methods, you can simply purify it with the power of your own breath.

Polished aventurine

Polished kunzite

Polished larimar

CRYSTAL FACTS

WHAT CLEANSER TO USE: your own breath

QUALITIES OF CLEANSER: sending an intention with your breath can remove negativity

Rough snow quartz

Rough azurite

The breath method
Take a few deep breaths and clear your mind. Pick up your crystal and focus on removing any negativity it holds, saying to yourself: "I cleanse this crystal with love." Breathe in deeply and exhale forcefully on it. Visualize any bad energy that comes off it being absorbed by the ground and changed by Mother Earth into vibrant energy once more. For a large crystal, breathe into every facet or side of the crystal.

Re-energizing crystals with sunlight

Although this is not an essential process, it can be good to do when you first buy your crystals. The natural, fiery energy of the sun can boost the crystal's own subtle vibrations so that they work at their highest power.

The sun method

To re-energize your crystals they need to be in full sunlight for about 24 hours. On a sunny day, place your crystals on the outside of a sunny windowsill (glass reduces the sun's strength) in the early morning and take them in at dusk; repeat on the next sunny

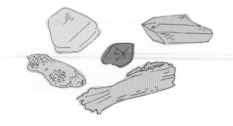

day. Alternatively leave them out in your garden covered by a linen cloth. However, do not place crystal balls in the sunlight, as this poses a fire risk.

Alternative methods

You can also energize crystals in moonlight, putting them out at night and retrieving them in the morning; try to choose a particular phase such as a new or full moon. The more emotional moon energizes in a gentle, subtle way, suiting the opaque stones such as agates, moonstones, and obsidians.

CRYSTAL FACTS

WHAT ENERGIZER TO USE: sunlight

QUALITIES OF ENERGIZER: sunlight is a natural energizer

CRYSTALS NOT TO BE ENERGIZED IN FULL SUNLIGHT: amethyst, aquamarine, aventurine, beryl, celestite, heat-treated citrine, fluorite, kunzite, lapis lazuli, malachite, opal, rose quartz, tourmaline, turquoise, as they can fade or be adversely affected by the heat

Polished sunstone

Polished red garnet

Polished translucent moonstone

Polished labradorite egg

Dedicating your crystal

Rough gold calcite

Rough purple fluorite

Rough blue apatite

Polished turquoise

Before you start working with your newly cleansed crystal it is a good idea to dedicate it. This simple empowerment can make a big difference to how well your crystal will work for you; it literally "turns on" its special vibrational frequency, making sure it works on the right wavelength. Making a special dedication ensures that the crystal works for the highest good of all the people concerned.

The dedication method
Hold each crystal individually in your hands, visualize it surrounded with white light, and say out loud: "I am going to use this crystal for the best and highest intentions." Now move on to the attuning process on page 156.

Rough pink tourmaline

CRYSTAL FACTS
WHAT CRYSTALS TO USE: all the new crystals that you have cleansed

Polished red tiger's eye

Polished carnelian

Polished amethyst

Attuning (or programming) your crystals

Rough sodalite

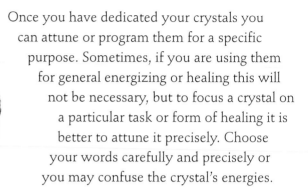

Polished hematite

Rough blue tourmaline

Polished chiastolite

Once you have dedicated your crystals you can attune or program them for a specific purpose. Sometimes, if you are using them for general energizing or healing this will not be necessary, but to focus a crystal on a particular task or form of healing it is better to attune it precisely. Choose your words carefully and precisely or you may confuse the crystal's energies.

The attuning method

Pick up your first crystal to attune for the tip you have chosen to do in the book. Think carefully about your intention, about the area you want to change, or how the crystal can cure or have a stimulating influence. Formulate the exact words in your head, such as: "I intend this crystal to protect my entrance" or "I intend this crystal to help cure my headaches." When you are sure of your intention, take your crystal in your hands and sense its energy. When you feel spiritually connected, speak your intention in a clear voice. Say it two or three times to fix it firmly in the crystal. Let yourself be open to your higher wisdom and any guidance it gives you. When you intuitively feel the intention is locked in your crystal, put it down and move away from it. To use an attuned crystal for another purpose, you will need to cleanse it and reprogram it.

CRYSTAL FACTS
WHAT CRYSTALS TO USE: all your new crystals that you have dedicated (see page 155)

Polished opaque moonstone

Choosing and dedicating a crystal as a gift

If you are buying a crystal as a gift for someone, hold an image of them in your mind or mentally say their name as your walk around the crystal shop. Handle different crystals, feeling their shape and energy, until one seems to resonate well with your friend's image or name. Turn it over a few times in your hand to make sure its vibrations are right, and you are happy with the stone.

Attuning the crystal

At home, cleanse your chosen crystal (see pages 149–153), then pick up and hold it firmly in your hands until you feel its subtle pulsations. Ask it to keep your friend safe and secure and to work for his or her highest good. Do not try to impose any of your views about how any of their characteristics could be improved. Give the stone to this person with your highest regard and with love.

Polished rhodochrosite

CRYSTAL FACTS
WHAT CRYSTAL TO USE:
your gift crystal that you have cleansed (see pages 149–153)

Glossary/Index

ACKNOWLEDGMENTS

I would like to thank Liz Dean for her support and creative input on this book. Also my thanks go to Jerry Goldie for his inspired design and Trina Dalziel for her attractive illustrations. As always a big thanks to my sister Gill for her love and positive encouragement and to all my friends, particularly Anna, Paul, Claire, Matt, and Janet, for their support as I wrote this book.

Mary Lambert is based in Shoreham-by-sea in West Sussex and can be contacted for reiki treatments and occasional Feng shui consultations on mary.lambert8@gmail.com.

PUBLISHER'S ACKNOWLEDGMENTS

Many thanks to to Philip Permutt of The Crystal Healer who provided invaluable information and to Charlie's Rock Shop, London, for supplying many of the crystals shown within these pages.

The Crystal Healer
www.thecrystalhealer.co.uk

Charlie's Rock Shop
www.charliesrockshop.co.uk

Jewelry featured on pages 77 and 78 made by Linda Jones; photographs by Jacqui Hurst.

FURTHER READING

The Book of Crystal Healing, Liz Simpson, Gaia, 1997
Crystals and Crystal Healing, Simon Lilly, Select Editions, 1998
Crystals for Health, Home and Personal Power, Ken and Joules Taylor, Collins & Brown, 1999
The Illustrated Guide to Crystals, Judy Hall, Godsfield, 2000
Crystal Healing, Cassandra Eason, Foulsham, 2002
Crystal Healing, Roger Croxson, Hodder Arnold, 2003
Cunningham's Encyclopedia of Crystal, Gem and Metal Magic, Llewellyn, 2003
The Crystal Bible, Judy Hall, Godsfield, 2003
The Power of Gems and Crystals, Soozi Holbeche, Piatkus, 2003